Contents

List of figures and tables

Acknowledgements

We are grateful to the Nuffield Foundation, which funded this study, and to the many policy-makers and analysts who have contributed, especially the 'key players' who were interviewed, the participants in two seminars held as part of the review, and those who provided information and access to work in progress, or read earlier drafts of this paper.

Helen Barnes
Patricia Day
Natalie Cronin

Note

Throughout this paper the terms 'resident parent' and 'non-resident parent' are used to denote parents living in the same or a different household from a child in respect of whom child support is due.

Amounts of child support payable in other countries have been converted to pounds sterling by the use of Purchasing Power Parities. These stabilise the fluctuations of exchange rates and take account of the cost of living in different countries. Purchasing Power Parities are developed and published by the OECD in its *Main Economic Indicators* series, published monthly.

Trial and error:

a review of UK child support policy

Helen Barnes, Patricia Day
and Natalie Cronin

Occasional Paper 24

FAMILY POLICY STUDIES CENTRE

Published by Family Policy Studies Centre
9 Tavistock Place, London WC1H 9SN

Tel: 0171-388 5900
Fax: 0171-388 5600

ISBN 1-901455-08-4

November 1998

British Library Cataloguing-in-Publication Data
A catalogue record for this book is available from the British Library

The Family Policy Studies Centre is an independent body which
analyses family trends and the impact of policy. It is a centre of
research and information. The Centre's Governing Council represents a
wide spectrum of political opinion, as well as professional, academic,
church, local authority and other interests. This Occasional Paper, like
all those in the series, represents the views of the authors and not
necessarily those of the Family Policy Studies Centre.

The Nuffield Foundation is a charitable trust established by Lord
Nuffield. Its widest charitable object is 'the advancement of social well-
being'. The Foundation's Child Protection and Family Law and Justice
Committee has supported this project to stimulate public discussion
about the important issues raised by child support policy. The views
expressed are, however, those of the authors and not necessarily those
of the Foundation.

Cover photographs by Format Photographers
Design and print by Intertype

Foreword

No policy initiative affecting families has excited more public and political hostility, or more media attention, than the Child Support Act, and its administrative arm, the Child Support Agency. Indeed this major attempt at social engineering has, together with the Poll Tax, become notorious; viewed as a failed policy initiative of the Thatcher era, created in indecent haste to satisfy political imperatives, and destined to cause far more problems than it solved. But is this an accurate impression?

The Family Policy Studies Centre has been involved at all stages of the debate about child support in Britain. It was one of the few family organisations in Britain to urge caution, and raise doubts about some of the proposals, at the time the initial policy was being formulated in the early 1990s (Burghes, 1991) and it has continued to monitor developments since. This, together with the fact that FPSC is concerned with the impact of policies on *all* families, makes it well placed to review the development and implementation of the policy, and to ask why it went so horribly and publicly wrong. *Trial and Error* is our account of the history of this policy. In it we both analyse the complex reasons for the failure of the child support policy and suggest directions for its future development. In addition to considering issues specific to this policy, we also identify more general lessons for the policy-making process. Drawing on interviews with thirty people who were most closely involved in the formulation, development and implementation of the policy, *Trial and Error* shows that concerns about the effects of the policy were voiced prior to and during its introduction, but that some of the issues which arose were different from those which had been identified in the early stages, and that the political climate did not, in any case, allow of substantial changes to the policy. A key factor here was the apparent parliamentary consensus on this issue which made any real debate impossible.

From its inception, organised opposition to the Child Support Act has highlighted the success of aggrieved men in dominating the policy agenda, whereas lone parents and their organisations have tended to find themselves sidelined in the debate. The complexities of designing a policy which is seen to be fair for all those involved – lone parents, non-resident parents, those with second families to support as well as other families as tax payers – have been lost among the sound and fury of competing interest groups. And, of course, some groups are better represented in this process than others.

Other countries have also grappled with these issues, and we know that British policy-makers did seek to learn lessons from abroad when drawing up the child support policy. Systems in Australia, New Zealand, and the USA were studied in the run-up to the design and implementation of UK policy, but the experience of other European countries does not appear to have influenced policy development. Yet in many countries within the European Union, the issue of child support has generated little comparable public hostility. In many cases there is general acceptance of the need to support children, both through parental contributions and by generous state support and services for families. Several countries have successfully implemented payment formulas, although few have taken contentious cases entirely out of the hands of the court system.

Trial and Error looks briefly at what we can learn from our European neighbours, as well as considering the more recent developments in the USA and Australia. In this way we seek to open up the debate by comparing key features of child support systems in eight countries, and analysing the strengths and weaknesses of contrasting approaches to issues such as the calculation, enforcement and administration of maintenance.

It is clear that the need for an effective child support policy has in no way diminished since the early 1990s. The number of children living in one-parent households has continued to rise, and poverty is still the overwhelming experience of such families. But, as we show, child support cannot be detached from the wider structures of financial and practical support for families. Whilst the payment of maintenance, effectively enforced, can deliver an important source of income for lone parents and their children, the amounts can never be enough to support a family for the simple reason that more and more families need at least one and a half pay packets to 'get by': two families, each with their own household costs, cannot effectively be supported by one, or even two earners.

The wider economic consequences of family breakdown are beyond the scope of this study. What is clear, however, is that the growing poverty experienced by parents and children in lone-parent families can only be tackled effectively by a multi-faceted approach. In the short term, this must deliver more child maintenance and better employment opportunities for lone parents, but it also needs to address the much larger question of what it is that makes such a high proportion of British parents separate.

Ceridwen Roberts
Director

1 Introduction

As long ago as 1974, the Finer Committee on Lone-Parent Families identified the need to assimilate the functions of what were referred to as the 'three systems' of family law: divorce courts, magistrates' courts and the administration of social security benefits. The recommendation was for the creation of an administrative mechanism which would calculate maintenance and bring together private obligation and public entitlement. There was little enthusiasm for this proposal at the time: both the perceived costs of such an enterprise, and the lack of political interest in the issue, meant that it was quickly consigned to obscurity (Davis *et al.*, 1998).

Since that time there have been immense changes in both the size and the composition of the lone-parent population, and there has also been a marked change in political and public attitudes; lone parents became the focus of a 'moral panic' about parenting and public expenditure during the late 1980s, and continue to have a high profile in the social policy debate.

Lone parents: a growing and changing population

The number of lone parents has grown rapidly over the past fifteen to twenty years, from a little over half a million in 1971 to over one and a half million in 1996. Figure 1.1

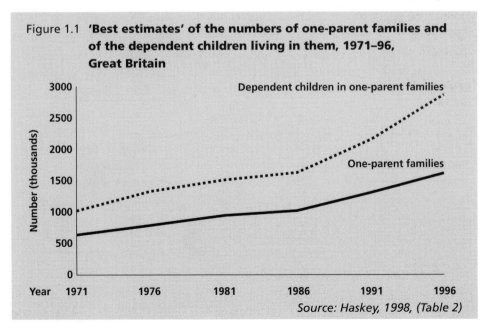

Figure 1.1 **'Best estimates' of the numbers of one-parent families and of the dependent children living in them, 1971–96, Great Britain**

Source: Haskey, 1998, (Table 2)

shows the overall growth in the numbers of lone parents and the numbers of children living in lone-parent households in Great Britain. Many more people than this will experience lone parenthood, either as a child or an adult, during their lifetime; it is estimated that between a third and a half of all UK children will spend part of their childhood in a lone-parent household (Ford *et al.*, 1995, Clarke, 1996).

It is not simply the number of lone parents which has grown: there have also been important changes in the composition and characteristics of the lone-parent population. The UK has the highest proportion of single (never-married) lone mothers in the European Union (Bradshaw *et al.*, 1996), although the growth in this category of lone parent is largely due to the increasing number of children being born to cohabiting couples who later separate (Burghes and Brown, 1995). Single (never-married) lone mothers pose particular challenges to child support policy and to lone-parent policy more widely, both because of their characteristics as a population (they are generally younger, and have younger children, than other lone mothers; they are less well-educated and have less work experience, all of which reduce their chances of finding employment) and because of the imprecise nature of the obligations their former partners may feel towards them and their children.

There are also differences in family size between single lone mothers and those who are separated or divorced: 70 per cent of single lone parents have only one dependent child, whereas over half of separated and divorced lone mothers have two or more dependent children (Office of Population Censuses and Surveys, 1993). However, the gap in family size has been reducing steadily in recent years (Haskey, 1998). This accounts for the sharp increase in the numbers of children living in one-parent households shown in Figure 1.1.

Although more people are experiencing lone parenthood, most people do not stay lone parents for long. Typically, an individual will only remain a lone parent for three to four years, although there is a minority of people who remain lone parents over a long period. There is, however, some evidence that the average duration of lone parenthood is increasing (Ford *et al.*, 1995).

The cost of lone parenthood

Both the rising numbers of lone parents and changes in their characteristics have led to large increases in public expenditure. Benefits for lone parents cost the taxpayer £1.3 billion in 1981-2 but this had risen to £4.3 billion in 1990-1, making it one of the fastest growing items in the social security budget. Lone parents also accounted for an increasing proportion of the budget. Numbers of lone parents in receipt of Income Support more than doubled from 330,000 in 1980 to 770,000 in 1989 (Supplementary Benefit/Income Support Annual Statistical Enquiries). By 1989 around 70 per cent of all lone parents were on Income Support (Ford *et al.*, 1995).

In common with other areas of growth in social security expenditure (Invalidity Benefit and Retirement Pension, for instance) the increasing cost of Income Support for lone parents is caused not only by more of them entering the benefit system, but also by fewer leaving. This is mainly because of lack of labour market demand, although one in seven lone mothers in the most recent survey (Ford et al., 1995) reported that either their own health or that of one of their children was a barrier to finding employment. However, less than half of all lone parents stay on benefit for two years or more: the majority stop claiming because they start work or increase their hours of work (Bradshaw and Millar, 1991).

There has been a fall in the proportion of lone mothers in employment. Table 1.1 shows the trends in the proportions of mothers working between 1979 and 1992.

Table 1.1 Lone mother and married/cohabiting mothers: percentage in full- and part-time work (Great Britain)

	1979/1981	1984/1986	1990/1992
Lone mothers full-time	23	18	17
Lone mothers part-time	25	24	24
Lone mothers: all	**49**	**42**	**42**
Married/cohabiting mothers: full-time	15	16	21
Married/cohabiting mothers: part-time	36	36	41
Married/cohabiting mothers: all	**52**	**52**	**63**

Source: OPCS, 1991

By 1990-2, only 42 per cent of lone mothers were in paid work, compared to 63 per cent of married or cohabiting mothers. Married and cohabiting mothers are likely to work part-time, particularly when their children are young. Working part-time is less likely to be economically viable for lone parents, as sole earners, especially where they have childcare costs. They therefore face a starker choice between full-time work and full-time motherhood (Ford et al., 1995).

Maintenance arrangements before the Child Support Agency

In addition to being less likely to have labour market income, lone parents at the end of the 1980s were also unlikely to be able to rely on maintenance as a source of income. This was due to a number of factors, including high levels of unemployment, changing legal practices in relation to the determination of maintenance awards (particularly 'clean break' settlements), and the inefficiency of maintenance collection by both the courts and the Department of Social Security. Half of all lone parents were receiving maintenance in 1979, but by 1989 this had fallen to 30 per cent, and was only 22 per cent amongst those receiving Income Support (Bradshaw and Millar, 1991). The Fowler reviews of the mid-1980s, which had identified the increased numbers of lone parents as a cause of rising social security expenditure, nonetheless made no recommendations regarding the recovery of maintenance in respect of lone parents.

Prior to the introduction of the Child Support Agency maintenance was dealt with by the courts, and by Liable Relative Officers (LROs) working for the Department of Social Security (DSS). Court awards of maintenance tended to be higher for divorced and separated lone parents than for those who were single (Department of Social Security, 1990, vol 2). The court system also had a tendency to be regressive as awards did not increase in line with income, and accounted for larger proportions of the incomes of the lowest paid non-resident parents. Lone parents claiming Income Support who were not receiving maintenance would be interviewed by a Liable Relative Officer, and maintenance was sought either as a voluntary payment or via the courts, based on the amount of benefit in payment. There is evidence that in times of staff shortage, LROs, who tended to be among the more experienced members of DSS staff, would be diverted from the task of pursuing maintenance to deal with backlogs of other work within the office. This was regarded as a key factor in the declining number of lone parents on benefit who received maintenance (National Audit Office, 1990).

Research evidence (Bradshaw and Millar, 1991; Ford et al., 1995) has consistently shown that those parents who are receiving maintenance are most likely to be in paid employment. One of the key objectives of the child support policy was to increase the number of lone parents in employment, by providing an income which could be supplemented by earnings. The relationship between maintenance and employment is not necessarily causal, however. Women who are employed tend to be more highly educated and stand to gain more by working. They receive maintenance mainly because their former partners are also well-educated people able to command good salaries. But maintenance has also been demonstrated to exert a small, but significant, independent effect in increasing the employment rates of all lone parents, even those with relatively few qualifications (Ford et al., 1995).

The White Paper, *Children Come First* (Department of Social Security, 1990), and the legislation which followed it, was introduced in a period which saw a focus on the welfare of children. The Children Act 1989 had established the principle that the child's welfare should be paramount, and was widely welcomed. The rhetoric surrounding child support was framed in similar terms, speaking of continuing commitment to children following relationship breakdown, although the resulting legislation was to define these responsibilities almost solely in terms of financial support.

By the time of its creation the Child Support Act had become accepted as a necessity, and its introduction met with all-party support. Yet this ambitious policy initiative was to prove both extremely controversial and hugely inefficient. Why did a policy which appeared to enjoy widespread support fail so spectacularly?

In its assessment of the difficulties of maintenance assessment, payment and collection the White Paper did not appear to take full account of the various demographic, economic and social factors which were involved. More recently, the Social Security Select Committee (SSSC), in concentrating on the difficulties of policy implementation, also appears to have neglected the importance of social and economic changes, and their effects on public attitudes to the legitimacy of child support policy:

'The experience of the Child Support Agency shows that even when policy and legislation has broad cross-party support in Parliament, that policy can come close to being frustrated and derailed by over-hasty implementation and poor levels of administrative performance'. Fifth SSSC Report, 1996-7 session, pxi

This review considers both the formulation and implementation of the Child Support Act, drawing on interviews with those who were key players in the design and implementation of policy, as well as on a wide range of documentary material in the public domain. In particular, it seeks to analyse to what extent the problems which arose were, or could have been, foreseen. The effectiveness of the policy is evaluated, not only in terms of the Government's objectives, but in terms of its effects on the lives of those who were supposed to benefit: parents and children.

The policy ran into difficulty for at least four inter-related reasons. These are:
- structural problems arising from what the policy set out to do;
- implementation difficulties because of the way it was introduced;
- frustration with the administration of the policy;
- a failure of marketing to establish the legitimacy of the policy aims.

Britain is, of course, by no means alone in facing the issue of child support, in a context of changing family structure throughout the developed world. Policies adopted in Europe, Australia, and the USA provide evidence of the wide range of options available both in terms of issues of principle and systems of administration. Whilst overseas experience did inform the development of UK child support policy, it is arguable that the countries selected were not fully representative of the range of child support systems which exist, and that the analysis of the systems observed may not have been sufficiently rigorous. This review takes a systematic approach to the comparison of child support regimes. Chapter Two provides an account of the development and implementation of the policy based on published data. Chapter Three draws on the accounts of thirty people who were key players in the process, who were interviewed for the review, to identify the forces which shaped the policy. Chapter Four outlines models of child support, and compares key features of the systems adopted in practice. Information on child support in eight countries is also provided in a standard format.

In addition to providing a case study of child support legislation, this review also provides broader insights into the process of public policy-making. Chapter Five considers the lessons which can be drawn for the future development of child support in the UK, whilst Chapter Six analyses the implications for policy-making more generally.

2 The development of the policy

The White Paper, *Children Come First*, was published in October 1990 (Department of Social Security, 1990). It argued that any system of maintenance should ensure that parents honour their legal and moral responsibilities to maintain their children wherever they could afford to do so. It contained four main proposals:

- The establishment of a **formula** for the assessment of child maintenance (see next page).
- The creation of the **Child Support Agency.** This was to be established as a 'Next Steps' Agency under the authority of the Secretary of State for Social Security. The tasks of the Agency were to trace absent parents, investigate parents' means, and assess, collect and enforce payment of child maintenance.
- The introduction, in April 1992, of a **maintenance disregard** of £15 per week for means-tested benefits other than Income Support.
- A change in the **definition of full-time work** for benefit purposes from 24 to 16 hours per week, enabling people to move from Income Support to Family Credit.

What finally created the impetus for the policy is not clear. The publication, by the Labour Party, of a consultation document on the enforcement of maintenance orders on New Year's Day 1990 may have played a part, but there appears to be widespread agreement that Mrs Thatcher's now famous speech to the National Children's Home later that month was crucial, not only in spurring civil servants into developing a new policy framework, but in defining the non-payment of maintenance as a moral failure by fathers. This latter aspect may have had contradictory effects. On the one hand, it created an apparent consensus which muted debate about the principles of the legislation amongst politicians and interest groups, whilst on the other, it may have increased hostility to the policy amongst fathers, who were being branded as feckless.

It is known that around 90 responses from pressure groups were received during the consultation period, which ended in January 1991. An analysis of these responses (Davis *et al.*, 1998) reveals that the vast majority supported the principle of a non-resident parent's ongoing financial responsibility for children, and of a formula to assess maintenance. However, there was almost universal concern about the specific formula proposed, which was regarded as inflexible, and likely to create hardship for non-resident parents and second families. Many responses also expressed opposition to the reduction in benefit as a penalty for resident parents who refused to co-operate with the new procedures, an issues which was later to dominate the Parliamentary process (Davis *et al.*, 1998). Only two organisations, Church Action on Poverty and the National Council for One Parent Families, explicitly favoured the creation of the Child

The Maintenance Formula

Calculating the amount of maintenance involves five elements:

The maintenance requirement

This represents the baseline calculation of maintenance. It is based on the Income Support amounts for the parent with care and children. Maintenance may be paid below this level (if the absent parent has insufficient income to meet the maintenance requirement) or at a higher level. The main significance of this first calculation is that the absent parent must pay 50 per cent of his assessable income (see below) until the maintenance requirement figure has been met. After this point, the rate of deduction is reduced.

Exempt income

Exempt income represents the minimum amount allowed for the day to day expenses of the absent parent. This is also based on Income Support rates. It includes amounts for the absent parent and any of his own children who are living with him, but does not include amounts for a new partner or any stepchildren.

Assessable income

This is the amount of a parent's income left after the deduction of exempt income. Where there is no assessable income, a minimum payment may be required (see below).

Proposed maintenance

This is the actual amount that the absent parent will have to pay, unless paying it would reduce his income to below the level of protected income (see below). Absent parents with 'excess' assessable income after the maintenance requirement has been met pay a percentage of this income (up to a ceiling) which varies according to income and number of children.

Protected income

This final element of the formula ensures that the absent parent's income does not fall below a certain level. At this stage the presence of a new partner and stepchildren is taken into account (both their costs and their incomes).

Minimum payment

Originally £2.20 per week, now £5.10. This applies to people on Income Support or in cases where the formula produces an amount below the minimum. There are a number of exemptions, including cases where the absent parent is in prison, responsible for a child living with them under 16 (or 16 to 19 and in full-time education) or receiving certain disability benefits. The effect of this is that the minimum payment mainly applies to single men on income support.

Note: Details of the formula have been modified since its introduction, but the basic process is unchanged.

Support Agency, whilst those with existing involvement in maintenance arrangements, such as the courts and the Law Society, vigorously opposed this measure.

These criticisms appear to have had no significant influence on the Bill, which was published in February 1991, and was to remain virtually unchanged when it received Royal Assent on 25 July 1991, despite widespread criticisms from both within and outside Parliament.

> *'The many criticisms of the Bill and the Agency which have come from voluntary organisations working in the field express a unanimity of dismay that so ill-considered a project has reached the point of legislation.'* Lord McGregor, House of Lords Hansard 526, no 48, col 794.

A consultation document on the Regulations to be made was issued in November 1991. Over 100 responses to this document were received: these were never published and also appear to have had very little effect in shaping the Regulations (Davis *et al.*, 1998, Garnham and Knights, 1994). The Social Security Select Committee (SSSC, Second Report, 1990-91 session) which published its report while the Bill was having its Second Reading in the Lords, expressed grave reservations about the retrospective effect of the legislation, particularly with respect to existing 'clean break' settlements. It recommended that specific provision to cover these situations be drafted. Again, this was disregarded. Treasury pressures were suspected to lie behind the decision to overturn existing settlements, but may not have been as influential as they were thought to be at the time. This issue is discussed in more detail in Chapter 3.

The Bill's passage through Parliament

It is noteworthy that the Child Support Bill was introduced in the House of Lords, rather than the House of Commons, a procedure normally reserved for non-controversial legislation. The reasons for this are not clear, but one motivation may have been to allow lawyers in the Upper House, who were likely to have objections to several of the proposed changes, an opportunity to debate them. Overall, the House of Lords appears to have taken the more critical approach, but the Child Support Bill received a minimum of scrutiny, passing through both Chambers in less than twenty hours of debate (Davis *et al.*, 1998). Some of the problems which arose later were, however, anticipated at this stage.

During the Second Reading of the Bill in the House of Lords, there was widespread acceptance of the principle of upholding the absent parent's obligation to pay, and for enforcing the payment of maintenance. Lord Houghton was the sole dissenting voice. His views, which were dismissed as eccentric, now appear to have been extremely prescient:

> *'People should be allowed to make fresh starts to their lives. Children cannot come first all the time while mothers and fathers have to reconstruct their own lives and try to get something from them. We are saying that children should come first so we should put them first. We shall have to discard a good deal of conventional thinking about parental obligations.'* House of Lords Hansard 526, vol 48, col 815.

Concern was expressed about the constitutional implications of the Bill. Lord Mishcon referred to it as a *'legislative skeleton'* and was highly critical of the fact that only 12 of 94 Regulations which fell to be made would require affirmative resolution by Parliament. Of particular concern were the precise circumstances which would exempt a parent with care from the obligation to co-operate, the effects on arrangements regarding the family home, the powers of Child Support Inspectors, and whether appeals would be heard by tribunals (for which Legal Aid is not available) or by courts. Clause 22 requiring resident parents to co-operate or forfeit a proportion of their benefit was removed by the Lords but was reinstated by the Government when the Bill returned to the Lower House. The question of whether the creation of a new Agency represented the best option was raised by several people; many would have preferred to see a family court, as had been recommended by the Finer Committee, whilst others argued that providing adequate resources for Liable Relative work might be sufficient to improve collection rates (House of Lords Official Report 25.2.91).

Introduction of the Child Support Agency

The Child Support Agency (CSA) opened its doors to the public on 5 April 1993. It was responsible for all new cases of child maintenance from that date. The cases of those already separated at that date were to be taken on in instalments over the following four years. From 6 April 1997 it was planned that the CSA would be fully operational and deal with all child maintenance applications. The take-on of cases with existing maintenance arrangements was subsequently deferred indefinitely because of the outstanding caseload, reinforcing the public view of the Agency as a residual system for those on benefits.

The Child Support Agency costs in the region of £110 million per year to run. It was set a target of saving £530 million in social security benefits during its first year of operation (SSSC, First Report, 1993-4 Session), a sum which as we shall see, was to create huge pressures on the Agency, and in fact took three years to achieve. In setting up the CSA, it had been envisaged that the Agency would function mainly as a broker between parents, rather than having a large role in the collection of maintenance. This has proved to be an unrealistic expectation, unsurprisingly, since over three-quarters of payments had been made to the courts or the DSS (rather than direct to the lone parent) under the previous system (Department of Social Security, 1990).

Evidence of emerging problems

Six months after the introduction of the CSA, hostile reactions had begun to emerge both in the press and in constituents' correspondence with MPs. Eight hundred letters were received by the Social Security Select Committee, leading to the first of what were to become numerous enquiries into the workings of the Agency. Pressure groups, such as Families Need Fathers, already in existence, and the National Campaign for Child Support Action (NACSA), formed specifically in response to the Child Support Act, proved highly effective in gaining media coverage for their opposition to the policy.

The main concerns at that time related to the formula, in particular its treatment of pre-existing 'clean break' settlements, travel to work costs, costs arising from contact visits to children, debts arising from marriage or separation, and the inescapable costs of caring for stepchildren (SSSC, First Report, 1993-4 Session). In contrast to the debate before the Agency was set up, which had focused on lone parents, these protests were coming from the men who were affected by the Act. This appears to have taken members of the Committee by surprise:

> *'Do you not think it is extraordinary how so much of the argument in the run up to implementation of this legislation was about the mother being in some way under threat and how the debate since implementation is almost entirely focused on the completely different question of the absent parent paying their maintenance?* David Willetts, SSSC, First Report, 1993-4 Session, Evidence p18-9

In addition to objections to the content of the policy, there were a large number of administrative problems involved in its implementation, which further undermined public support. These included delays, incorrect assessments and incorrect handling of confidential data. The First Report of the Chief Child Support Officer found that the amount of the assessment and the adjudication process itself were correct in only 14 per cent of cases, and that 39 per cent of assessments were incorrect. The report of an independent adjudicator, published in 1995, showed that of 1,380 cases examined, only half had correct maintenance assessments, and only one in seven had been dealt with according to the approved procedure for calculating payments (Journal of Social Policy, 24(2)). Concern about financial procedures was also evinced by the Comptroller and Auditor General, who qualified the 1994-5 CSA accounts, after finding only 47.5 per cent of maintenance orders 'demonstrably correct' (Child Support Agency, 1995). The Data Protection Registrar received 206 complaints against the CSA in 1994, the largest number ever made concerning a single data user (The Guardian, 22.7.95). As Chapter 6 discusses, the sheer scale of the problems was magnified by the fact that the Agency was operating within new structures of accountability.

By August 1994, there were 2,412 appeals waiting to be heard, compared with 414 in January of that year (Council on Tribunals, 1995). A report published by five national children's charities (Clarke *et al.*, 1994), based on a small sample of non-working lone mothers, argued that the intervention of the CSA had caused conflict with former partners and emotional damage to children in a large number of cases. The Social Security Committee's second report into the operation of the CSA was published in November 1994. It made over twenty recommendations for changes in the policy, including the adoption of standard housing amounts, recognition of informal arrangements and past settlements and changes in the effective dates of assessments. In January 1995 the DSS published both its response to that report, and the White Paper *Improving Child Support*, which contained important changes to the original scheme, including changes to the effective date of assessment and the introduction of a discretionary 'departures' scheme.

A Client Satisfaction Survey undertaken for the DSS by MORI in 1994 (Speed and Kent, 1995) was narrowly focused on issues of service delivery, rather than the content of policy. As one would expect, levels of satisfaction were generally low, and delays in assessment and lack of response to letters were common sources of complaints. Over-all, resident parents tended to be more satisfied with the level of service than non-resident parents.

Responding to the crisis

A number of administrative strategies were pursued by the Child Support Agency in trying to deal with the backlog of cases which mounted up during the initial months of the scheme. Many of them had a negative impact on public perceptions of the Agency. They included moving between 'case-management' (person-based) and 'production-line' (task-based) processing of cases, prioritising cases where information was readily available and an emphasis on making maintenance assessments rather than enforcing their payment once made (Davis *et al.,* 1998). The strategy of pursuing 'soft targets' where maintenance was already in payment was one which proved particularly contentious, and played a major role in undermining the legitimacy of the policy, but was probably inevitable given the unrealistic financial targets which had been set (Clarke *et al.,* 1996). The practise of setting punitively high Interim Maintenance Assessments (IMAs) in cases where non resident parents did not provide information also created great opposition.

Staff management during this initial period was widely regarded as poor; many of those recruited had no prior experience of the type of work involved. This had been a deliberate strategy. Rather than re-training existing Liable Relative Officers, who had experience in dealing with maintenance, the plan was for a fresh start aimed at fostering new attitudes to the assessment and collection of child support. However, the combination of new staff and new legislation proved a difficult one, and it became necessary to call upon the experience of Liable Relative Officers to clear the backlog of cases after the first six months.

Modifications to the original child support scheme were suggested at a conference hosted by the Child Poverty Action Group in May 1994. At this stage, Sue Slipman, then Director of the National Council for One-Parent Families, was opposed to making too many changes as she felt the CSA had yet to pursue maintenance with any degree of vigour. It was also felt that the concessions which were being proposed tended to favour absent fathers at the expense of resident parents. Changes were also recom-mended in the first Social Security Select Committee report on the Agency. Ros Hepplewhite, then Chief Executive of the Child Support Agency, was reluctant to make judgements in view of the short period of time which had elapsed. There was also some reluctance by members of the Committee to 'complicate the formula' (sic) SSSC, First Report, 1993-4 Session, Evidence, p34)

The effectiveness of the Agency

The CSA was supposed to increase the number of maintenance awards in payment but, as Table 2.1 shows, the *overall* proportion of lone parents who reported receiving maintenance remained unchanged during the first two years of the Child Support Agency's operation. Moreover, although the proportion of single (never-married) moth-

Table 2.1 **Reported receipt of maintenance by lone parents, 1989-1994 (%)**

	1989 %	1991 %	1993 %	1994 %
Single (never-married) mothers	14	12	23	14
Previously cohabiting mothers	14	25	23	26
Divorced mothers	40	46	43	45
Separated mothers	32	33	31	32
Lone fathers	3	9	10	16
All (excluding widows)	**29**	**30**	**30**	**30**

Source: Marsh et al., 1997

ers who reported receiving maintenance (a group poorly served by the previous Liable Relative arrangements) almost doubled in 1993, it had returned to its previous level by the following year.

Marsh *et al.* conclude that CSA assessments had a neutral effect for the following reasons:

- assessments were made in cases where maintenance was already in payment;
- assessments were made in cases where maintenance would have been paid anyway;
- assessments were made in cases where absent parents were exempt from payment;
- assessments were made in cases where payment would not have been made under the previous system, and were still not being made.

Thus an increase in the overall volume of payments can be achieved only once this last category of assessments is successfully enforced.

A key aim behind the policy had been not only to increase the **number** of maintenance awards in payment, but to increase the average **level** of maintenance paid. Prior to the introduction of child support, the average amounts paid had been £15.00 per week if arranged by the DSS or Magistrates' Court, £20.00 if arranged by the County Court and £24.00 if arranged by the Scottish Courts (Department of Social Security, 1990, Vol 2). The child support legislation aimed to increase average weekly payments to something more in the region of £40.00 to £50.00 (House of Commons Hansard Oral Answers 30.11.92). Table 2.2 shows the average full maintenance assessments made under the Child Support Act.

It can be seen that the level of maintenance awards fell after March 1995, reflecting policy changes which came into effect in April of that year, and that the average for all full assessments has now fallen back to around the original pre-child support level (Department of Social Security, 1997). Whilst the amounts payable by those in employment have risen under the new system, the large number of non-resident parents with a zero assessment (because they are on benefit or a low income) depresses the average.

Table 2.2 **Average weekly full maintenance assessments**

	Where absent parent in paid employment	All full assessments
June 1994	£45.53	£27.06
October 1994	£44.34	£26.39
March 1995	£43.46	£25.56
August 1995	£38.66	£23.37
February 1996	£38.62	£22.86
August 1996	£38.02	£22.02
February 1997	£37.73	£21.39

Source: House of Commons Written Answers 7 July 1997, col 374

By May 1996, three years after the introduction of the Agency, only about one third of lone parents receiving Income Support or Family Credit had received an assessment (SSSC, Fifth Report, 1995-6 Session). A large number of cases (150,845 in the first nine months of 1996-7 alone) had been cleared without assessment. These included cases where it was accepted that the resident parent had good cause not to co-operate with the Agency, where the absent parent was not known, could not be traced, was abroad, had died, or was in prison. The 'good cause' provisions came to be regarded by the Agency as a major weakness in the system: it was thought that lone parents were too easily able to obtain exemption by describing difficult circumstances (Department of Social Security, 1996a). Following commissioned research into Child Support Officers' decision-making processes (Provan *et al.*, 1996), new procedures aimed at developing a more probing interview style amongst Child Support Officers have been implemented. A pilot project which involves lone parents being interviewed about child support at the start of their benefit claim (as was traditional practice for the Liable Relative Officers) has also been extended nationwide.

Collusion with former partners, leading to refusal to co-operate, is also generally regarded as widespread (Bradshaw, 1996, Davis *et al.*,1998), although this is disputed by other sources (SSSC, Fourth Report, 1995-6 Session). In late 1995, it was announced that the benefit penalty for refusing to co-operate was to be increased by over 100 per cent (Department of Social Security, 1995). This was implemented in October 1996: the penalty is now renewable rather than a 'once only' sanction (Department of Social Security 1996b; CPAG, 1998).

This chapter has documented some of the many problems encountered in the development and implementation of child support policy from the perspective of events in the public domain; Chapter 3, by contrast, draws on the experiences of those who were most heavily involved in these processes.

3 Key player recollections of the making of the child support system

Looking at the past history of a policy

Some government policies, particularly the more contentious ones, tempt analysts into detailed detective work. Child support policy is such a case. It is known that in the period between 1990 and 1994 child support policy and its implementation developed a high and hostile public profile. This research sought to discover how and when it became a contentious issue: why the maintenance of children became a controversial policy at the end of the 1980s.

The chaotic progress of this policy is not only interesting in its own right, but may also be taken as a representative example of unpopular policy-making generally in the UK. The aim was to discover if there are insights to be gained from problematic policies which could be used to avoid future pitfalls, and to see whether hindsight has any place in the modification of longstanding Whitehall policy-making traditions. In short, the review asked what lessons could be learned from past policy mistakes. This question is addressed in more detail later in this chapter.

To these analytical ends, a number of politicians, civil servants and others involved with the early development of the policy were asked to give their own account of what happened. This chapter is based on interviews and conversations with people who were key policy participants in the late 1980s and early 1990s. It is an analysis of how they remembered the issues, aims and operation of child support policy. Naturally their accounts were based mainly on freely admitted hindsight, but they were also aided by reference to documents written at the time.

Thirty people were interviewed over a period of four months during late 1997 and early 1998. Four people who were asked to participate refused to talk, for a variety of reasons. The refusals were not confined to one category of interviewee, and those interviewed represent a broad cross-section of the people involved in child support policy in the ten years from about the mid-1980s up to 1995. Politicians, lobby groups and civil servants were well represented. Both insiders – people making policy – and outsiders – people working with the results of policy – were interviewed. No users of the system were knowingly interviewed, although it became obvious that some inter- viewees were speaking with a degree of personal experience and involvement; at least, some experience of single parenthood and child support if not of the Agency itself. To an extent, lobby groups were used as proxies for direct users.

The people interviewed included politicians and ex-politicians, two from the House of Lords and the rest from the House of Commons. Of the politicians still with seats, there was one Liberal Democrat, two were Labour and three were Conservatives. Civil servants and ex-civil servants from the DSS were interviewed, as well as three Treasury officials. In addition, people from three interest and lobby groups, the Law Society, several public watchdogs and various interested and specialist academics took part.

Interview topics were decided following discussions with experts in lone parent and social security policy, and the interviews were carried out entirely on a lobby basis with guarantees of confidentiality. The story told by the thirty people interviewed follows.

The triggers and drivers of the Child Support Act 1991

Interviewees had been involved with child support policy for varying lengths of time, people move on and around in the policy world. Both politicians and civil servants recalled, however, that lone parenthood and child support were minor, but growing, issues as far back as the late 1970s and the early 1980s.

During the early years, however, interest was largely confined to fact-finding. For example, in 1988 at a regular Junior Ministers' meeting, Mrs Thatcher asked Michael Portillo to investigate what was going on in situations where children were without parental financial support. At about this time a Labour and Liberal deputation raised a Parliamentary Question with the MP for St Albans on the disproportionate number of council houses being let to single parents in one constituency area.

Interest broadened as the Department of Social Security and the Treasury simultaneously studied the statistics on child maintenance. There was evidence that the courts were making meagre assessments and, moreover, failing to collect. The concern in Whitehall was expressed by senior civil servants thus:

> *'We had become aware of increasing numbers of lone parents by the mid-1980s. I remember the Chief Economist said to me "Just look at these figures, we should be worried about lone parents". This was in 1985. We all began to look at the numbers and the increasing numbers of single parents. We were worried at the time about the numbers on benefit and, more important, the numbers on low levels of maintenance. All in all, concern about low net incomes of single parents. I am certain the tone of the debate at this time was concern about children living within low income situations.'*

There was Parliamentary pressure for the issue to be sorted out. Requests for information at Ministerial meetings became demands for action. At one such meeting the Prime Minister was quoted as saying that something must be done and it must be done quickly and within that Parliament.

Civil servants at the Department of Social Security, and others, discussed and documented the inadequacies of the child maintenance systems operating at the time. The courts were proving to be an expensive and inefficient way of delivering very small amounts of maintenance to lone parents. The Department of Social Security's own maintenance collection scheme was criticised as similarly deficient.

> *'There had been great dissatisfaction with the Liable Relatives scheme and with the courts system for a long time. Finding an improved system was very*

important at the time. Neither the Liable Relatives Officers nor the courts were able to deliver maintenance payments satisfactorily. The courts were clogged up with cases waiting and settlements were delayed. This resulted in increased social security payments for women who had no incomes or low incomes because of delayed maintenance. Even where settlements were arrived at they were usually very low – small amounts of money.'

Ripples were being made by overseas policy observers, as one civil servant recalled:

'Some American called Garfinkel was at this time talking about the Wisconsin Scheme for child support and was attracting attention.'

Not everyone interviewed was clear about who had gone where and why some countries were selected for visits. Even those who went abroad on fact-finding missions to Australia and the United States could not always remember why particular places had been chosen, except that it was known on the policy grapevine that something interesting was happening:

'Countries visited before the UK child support legislation were picked out simply because we needed to find out about other systems and we knew that things were going on in other countries.'

It was generally a time of much civil service travel and exchange. Some senior civil servants accompanied politicians on trips abroad to find out about single parents and maintenance:

'We also saw that the lone parents issue was already happening in the USA in 1988-1989. In 1990 they were pursuing men to pay for the maintenance of their children. Here in the UK it was the culture that the State looked after children and people generally. We had had this culture since the Second World War, partly as a safety net for the unemployed.'

But according to interviewees, the thing which galvanised the child support issue came from the top of government in January 1990: it was the speech made by Mrs Thatcher at the George Thomas Society Annual Lecture at the Cafe Royal on Wednesday 17 January 1990 (Thatcher, 1990a).

'No father should be able to escape from his responsibility and that is why the Government is looking at ways of strengthening the system for tracing an absent father and making the arrangements for recovering maintenance more effective.'

The story is that this speech had followed examination of the Department of Social Security statistics on the size of maintenance default as well as press accounts of the scandal of absent fathers. Later in the year, in July 1990, Mrs Thatcher reinforced her pursuit of maintenance from absent parents when she gave the Pankhurst lecture to the 300 Group at the Savoy Hotel (Thatcher, 1990b). As befits a Pankhurst lecture, the Prime Minister's talk was about women, progress and families. Mrs Thatcher advocated a supportive attitude to lone-parent families under pressure for the sake of the children. But she also added that government had a role to make sure that this included helping parents to take financial responsibility for their children.

> *'Government too must be concerned to see parents accept responsibility for their children. For even though marriages may break down, parenthood is for life. Legislation cannot make irresponsible parents responsible. But it can and must ensure that absent parents pay maintenance for their children. It is not fair for them to expect other families to foot their bills too.'*

What had begun in the 1980s as a slow realisation by government and Whitehall that there were problems around maintenance for children, single parents and the social security system, became an urgent issue in 1990. What had started out as an intermittent interest in child support had become a concentrated policy activity by the beginning of the 1990s. The trigger to this fast gear-change, according to key players, was without doubt the Prime Minister. It was only slightly later, when policy-making was under way, that the Treasury became a key driver.

The forces behind the making of policy described here are not, however, unique to either child support or the Department of Social Security. It is quite common for Prime Ministers and the Treasury to combine their authorities to push along what they consider to be urgent and crucial policy. This heavyweight approach has been analysed recently in an ESRC funded study of the Treasury and Whitehall carried out by Nicholas Deakin and Richard Parry (Deakin and Parry, 1996/7).

> *'It is a key theme of British government that the Chancellor and the Prime Minister steer government policy.'*

A senior civil servant recalled the making of the child support and other policies during his thirty years of policy-making. His experiences were in tune with the findings of the academic study:

> *'Policy-making at this level of speed and intensity is almost always a product of the relationship between the Prime Minister and the Chancellor. This is the most significant political relationship. Where the Prime Minister is weak the voice of the Chancellor will prevail. And vice versa, where the Prime Minister is strong and the Chancellor is weak, the Prime Minister will assert authority. Where both are strong – as was the case in 1990 – then the relationship is formidable and policy is ploughed through.'*

The Treasury as a key policy driver?

To the extent that the Treasury, as well as the Department of Social Security, was concerned about the growth in the numbers of single parents who were dependent on the state for their income, it would not be unreasonable to assume that there was a special financial interest in the making of the UK child support policy. There is indeed some evidence that there was a Treasury line as well as a Department of Social Security line being held when the operation of the Agency was being outlined. But there is no evidence that the *idea* of the child support policy was inspired by notions of revenue gain:

> *'The reality of the child support policy was that it was going to reduce the social security bill. This was just a fact not a policy driver. What we must understand, however, is that all policy development in all government departments has an element of discussion about financial implications. This is not new and not unique to child support. It comes about naturally in meetings and discussions and the financial element is brought out by the economists and it is seen as their normal role in meetings.'*

Although interest in the financial returns on the policy kicked in later, the level of financial pressure from the Treasury was generally considered by most of the key players as about the norm for public policy-making at the time. This pressure was based on two main factors. First, there was the usual stringent line taken with high spending government departments. Second, and probably more significant, was the operational expectations of the newly created Next Steps Agencies. These Agencies were set up with more business-like structures than traditional public sector organisations and were expected to deliver services with performance and financial accountability. An ex-Department of Social Security officer recalled that the Child Support Agency, along with the other Next Steps Agencies, had to produce a business plan with a calculation of returns on investment as part of the new management of government. Business plans and operational strategies were, by the beginning of the 1990s, part of the culture of most public bodies, including NHS Authorities and Trusts.

The policy issue here, however, is not that the Treasury treated child support policy as a special case, but rather that it *should* have done. Taking a more flexible line with the new Agencies generally might have been more appropriate since these were, in a sense, experimental organisations. The Child Support Agency, in particular, was both new and had a difficult task to perform, and perhaps should not have had so much demanded of it. A Treasury official who was involved with the policy at the time suggested, with hindsight, that a softer Treasury line might have been more appropriate in April 1993:

> *'The Treasury and Revenue always ask "are we getting enough bang for buck here". They usually look to a return of 1:6 for most schemes and policies. The child support looked like it was going to be more of a 1:3 or 1:4 return. This was not enough for the Treasury. We were asked to get to the harder end of the calculation and aim for a return of 1:4 or 1:5.'*

Constructing the policy: speed and efficiency?

One of the accusations levelled against the child support policy-makers was that the whole exercise was carried out with indecent haste and that more time should have been allowed for consultation and reflection. It is true that civil servants and politicians in the Department of Social Security were given only four months (between February and June 1990) to come up with a policy. The account given by key players suggests, however, a more complex relationship between time allotted and end results. Moreover, they were far from clear that more time would have yielded better policy.

From the spring of 1990 policy work was at its height and a general framework was created. The policy-makers focused on the construction of a formula for calculating maintenance payments which, in the Department of Social Security tradition, allowed for minimum operational discretion, but although the bones of policy-making were in the Department of Social Security tradition, some of the latest ideas were included. For example, it was decided to start with a set of objectives based on the question 'what does fairness mean in the context of maintenance?'. In addition, the structures for both implementation and evaluation were incorporated. It was typically 1990s policy-making according to a key player at the Department of Social Security:

> 'Our job was to produce the implementation part of the child support policy. This was about delivering the policy as well as the other elements associated with implementing a new policy. For example, new policies have to be set within a good information system which will enable the policy to be evaluated. That is, to facilitate a flow of management information which can be fed back into a regular evaluation of performance and achievement of targets.'

At the same time, the financial arrangements and the public expenditure consequences were being scrutinised. The questions raised by the policy-makers were put into the White Paper published in October 1990 (Department of Social Security, 1990). The legal profession was consulted, and a public consultation period, originally until December 1990, was extended to January 1991. By usual policy-making standards this was a relatively short consultation period, but it was necessary in order to get the policy into the Bill stage by February 1991. The question remains as to whether a longer preparation and consultation period would have improved the policy or avoided some of the subsequent problems. The policy-makers thought not:

> 'All this was done in a tearing hurry but I maintain it was not done with inadequate reflection. It was all quite deliberate. High speed but high deliberation. The speed with which we worked made a difference to the quality of our lives not to the quality of the policy. We worked like the clappers for two years.'

It was suggested that it was not the speed of the policy-making which caused problems but rather the speed with which the Agency's operation was started up. We discuss this in more detail later in the chapter.

Problems and unpopularity: principle or practice?

Given that child support policy has become notorious, there has been much speculation as to which elements were most to blame: whether the policy principle itself was unpopular and, therefore, not a good idea; whether it was a good idea but suffered faulty construction and bad timing, and consequent unpopularity, or whether the problems lay neither in ideas nor construction but in implementation. This is not, however, a straightforward analytical question, for two main reasons. First, it is diffi-cult to separate out problems arising out of hostility to policy ideas and objectives from those which come from faulty manufacture and production. Second, even where the problems can be distinguished they may compound each other in a larger chaos. Although these are real dilemmas of analysis, it is necessary to distinguish intrinsic policy unpopularity from problems of construction and implementation if policy les-sons are to be learnt. What follows is an attempt to unpack and examine these problems, starting with the early ideas surrounding the policy.

According to key actors (and this is supported by documentary evidence from the time) the main tenets of child support policy were more or less universally accepted. They described the policy objective of parents, absent or otherwise, supporting their own children financially, as a proposition that few in government or anywhere else argued with at the time. The lobbies presenting with objections entirely on principle were, at the time of consultation, few and far between. Those groups opposed to the whole ethos of the policy argued that taking maintenance payments from absent fathers was an infringe-ment of the personal liberties of single women: being married to the State (as one Treasury Minister had described single parenthood) was seen as preferable to being married to men. As one of the interviewees who was part of this lobby remembered:

> 'We were against the principle of dependence of single parents on former partners for child support. We could also see practical contradictions between the benefit unit and the child support unit. We supported the principle of parents supporting their children – if it was possible, not as an over-riding principle of government.'

This was a view which did not appear to be widely shared by either politicians or public. Cross-party support at the time appeared seamless. It was not until much later that the Liberal Democrats declared their party line against the Agency and, to a degree, against the policy itself, on the grounds that it was anti-libertarian.

There are, however, a number of caveats to be noted in this context. First, policy rhetoric is often more attractive than the reality. And second, negative implications may not become apparent until certain stages of development are achieved. This is true of both the aims of the policy and its implementation. An illustration of the first proviso was given by a high ranking civil servant who detected an underlying disquiet during a Select Committee interrogation in 1991:

> 'It was obvious that the Select Committee did not think that the policy would work. While we expressed official optimism, the Select Committee expressed doubts.'

The questions asked were polite but searching, and although the discussion was mainly about the details of the formula, the tone of the proceedings became more uncertain about the policy as a whole as the session wore on. It was as if the initial All-Party ardour for the principle of the policy had cooled as the reality of what it would mean in practice became apparent.

Policy formulation as culprit?

If the straightforward principle of people supporting their own children financially was largely uncontested, the formula for assessing maintenance turned out to be less acceptable. As was suggested earlier, this unpopularity grew as people had time to think carefully about the implications of the policy. Between May 1992 and April 1993 more and more concerns were expressed about the content of the formula for assessing child support. Television programmes were made reflecting the objections of the lobby groups and suggesting that the policy contained elements which put women in danger. Mounting public hostility was fuelled by press reports highlighting the negative implications of extracting money from absent fathers. The irony was that the formula was intended to defuse controversy by its emphasis on fairness: in the event, it turned out to be seen as neither fair nor uncontroversial. Sensing that hostility to the policy was growing and might be getting out of hand, a senior minister called a meeting of Department of Social Security officials and politicians at the end of March 1993. In an attempt to effect reassurances, he set out the areas of criticism and concern:

> *'We began to realise that there was appearing what seemed to me some almighty flack. I alerted my colleagues in government generally and in the Department of Social Security as to what I saw as the flack looming up.'*

The meeting, which was designed to reassure policy-makers, did not. The timing was unfortunate, since it coincided with the commissioning of the Agency, which was an immediate disaster. If the formula had raised public doubts, then the Agency cemented them.

The Agency: a vehicle for disaster?

If child support policy had become increasingly unpopular as it developed on the drawing board, it fell into greater disrepute with the start-up of the Agency. Next Steps Agencies working at arm's length from Whitehall were intended to be efficient and effective service providers while having greater public accountability. The Child Support Agency immediately failed on all these counts: it was conceptually, organisationally and operationally untried. It started up with little idea of the nature and amount of work involved and, moreover, the wrong tools to carry it out; its staff were inexperienced and untrained; it set out in a great hurry to do an unknown job with an a computer system which proved to be inappropriate. However, in spite of all these negative factors, almost no one anticipated the sheer volume of the chaos. People interviewed recalled the disastrous beginnings of the Agency but, paradoxically, remembered expecting the system to work:

> *'At the start of the Agency there were pressures to get the thing up and rolling as quickly as possible. This was not unique to the Child Support Agency. This is very common in Department of Social Security policy-making. You get to the stage where it is going to happen and so you make it happen fast. We genuinely thought that the Agency was going to work.'*

'The Agency tried to do everything at once – a 'big bang' solution. It was doing assessment and enforcement, and both with maximum inefficiency. With hindsight we should have left assessment and concentrated on enforcement.'

The usual problems of policy implementation were exacerbated by the newly constructed Agency. The inexperienced workforce merely added weight to the already heavy workload, which had been unforeseen. A key player described how staffing problems put an extra strain on the system:

'The Agency started up in four or five centres and in at least two centres the staff came from organisations which had just closed down. These were not auspicious circumstances for recruiting staff.'

'New staff had no training, no experience, no targets and no idea about social security operational routine. They were not even given a broad-picture briefing. They did not even know about filing cases in alphabetical order so that they could be easily retrieved; the first lesson in bureaucratic training.'

Weighing the problems: the policy principle, the formula or the Agency?

The key players were all hard pressed to weigh the different elements in problems which dogged the child support policy. Most recalled a combination of things which conspired to bring chaos. Certainly the difficult start of the Agency's operation tipped the balance further towards public unpopularity and was an important contender for chief problem. The inclusion of past cases in the workload was another favourite for problem creation. This was not only branded as unfair practice but also added to the administrative chaos. Some key players thought that the pressure for a good financial performance from the Agency placed a great strain on the system: there were suggestions that the biggest problems were associated with the overly complex formula for assessment.

There were several interesting observations about the early public responses to the policy and the consequences of a face value acceptance of rhetoric. Speaking about the political debate in the House, one key player observed that universal agreement on a policy principle does not necessarily make for a successful policy – quite the reverse, in fact, in many cases:

'When everyone, including Ministers and officials, are very keen on a policy it is more likely to go wrong. Totally contrary to the accepted wisdom that controversy and lack of agreement make policy go wrong ... Within government everyone was very keen. On the surface, there was a disproportionate enthusiasm with Department of Social Security policy and cross-party support. The principle of the thing was undeniable – that all parents should be responsible for their children.'

Another key player remembered the House of Commons' response to the policy in its early stages:

> *'Looking back on the course of Parliamentary proceedings, I can say that the Bill was not adequately debated by MPs. There had been much lobbying by pressure groups but an amazingly large silence from MPs of all parties. The Whips had stitched it up. All politicians wanted the Act on the statute books. Between February 1991 and the Royal Assent in July 1991, politicians said very little. Just read Hansard to see how sparse were the comments in the House.'*

Recollections of some key players were precisely along these lines. They recalled that both politicians and civil servants were ingenuous about the child support policy in its early stages. The overwhelming silence of the Commons when the Bill was presented confirmed the policy-makers in their belief that there were no major objections: it was axiomatic that parents support their children. In the event, only one or two politicians foresaw, and spoke out about, the fury that would break loose once men realised the implications for themselves of the child maintenance formula.

Key players who cited the complexity of the formula as a major reason for its unpopularity and subsequent problems gave, at the same time, a justification for its complexity and choice. Traditional concepts of fairness enshrined in the social security system were part of the rationale behind the decision to go for a formulaic administrative approach instead of a discretionary, court-based, system: it was seen as the lesser evil in a range of possible alternative systems. The non-arbitrary rules of the social security system were assumed to be fairer and less divisive than courts' judgements on maintenance, in spite of the greater complexity and lack of transparency. Only one key player thought that child maintenance should have been left for the law to arbitrate, whereas most of the others could see no workable alternative to the Department of Social Security system:

> *'The failure of the Agency did not make anyone in my group suggest putting the system back into the courts. I am a lawyer and I did not think it a good idea to leave maintenance assessment and enforcement to the legal system.'*

If the key players were aware of the policy cost of a highly complex formula for assessment, they were not unaware of the problems associated, paradoxically, with a more simple approach to maintenance assessment:

> *'The complexity of the formula is intellectually extremely fair but the fairness was never transparent to the customers ... To have used a tax type system might have looked fairer because the tax system has a 'fair' image. But there would be big winners and big losers if child support was based on a percentage of earnings. A straightforward percentage system would lead to accusations of unfairness from other areas.'*

The retrospective effect of the formula was considered by many key players as one of the most significant reasons for the unpopularity of the policy:

> *'If you produce a new formula and you use it on people with already established arrangements then you are in trouble. The people aggrieved by the child*

support policy were those with small amounts of maintenance awarded in the past as part of divorce settlements.'

However, even those who saw this inclusion as an act of political and policy suicide were certain that it would have been 'unfair' to exclude it:

'It was seen as unfair to undo arrangements already in place. But it was seen also as unfair to allow old settlements, usually small amounts of maintenance, to remain in place. It was a no-win situation.'

It was impossible to divide the people interviewed neatly between 'problem camps'. They all talked about issues which covered the full range of formulation and implementation. It was difficult for key players to weigh the problems one against another; or to weigh the advantages of a simple formula against a complex one. It was also difficult to separate out policy unpopularity from inappropriate formulation and operations. Even with the benefit of hindsight, everything was fair and nothing was fair in the making of child support policy.

Could we have learned policy lessons from abroad?

One of the accusations levelled against child support policy-makers was that they failed to use other countries' experiences to inform their tasks. Certainly by the time the Agency got started, the academic community strongly favoured overseas models of child support in preference to the system in the UK. According to key players the lessons from overseas were somewhat more complex. There were, in addition, some notes of scepticism about learning policy lessons from abroad generally. With freely admitted hindsight some of the people interviewed remembered discovering that all was not perfect in child maintenance systems overseas. Sometimes glowing progress reports of other systems were brought back to the UK before they had revealed their operational flaws:

'We could have learned a bit more from Australia although they had problems – more than people talk about. Australia had problems with their Agency administration just like the UK. The Australians had problems actually collecting and handing over maintenance to caring parents: they had difficulties with resentful and difficult people – absent parents mainly.'

As the academic literature on cross-national policy studies has increasingly recognised, genuinely comparative analysis, in the sense of comparing like with like, is rare in both policy-making and in policy evaluation. Moreover, nationally specific elements may play an important role in the success or failure of a policy initiative. A key player reported similar lessons, about the importance of taking account of demographic and social structures, as well as cultural differences. For example, the nature of lone parenthood varies between countries as does its prevalence:

'In the mid to late 1980s, Australia shared, in essence, similar problems of single parents and their children unsupported by the absent parents. There

were, however, some demographic as well as policy differences between the two. First, there was nothing like the numbers of teenage and unmarried pregnancies in Australia as there was in the UK. The Australian problem was one of broken marriages, divorces and separations. The policy concern was with the children of broken marriages living without the financial support of the absent parent. Second, because the Australian benefits system was not as generous as in the UK, the lone parents and their children were seen as a child poverty issue. At the time of the child support legislation the housing benefit in Australia was non-existent. In contrast, the UK pre-legislation situation was a more generous benefits funding of lone parents, especially young single girls. In the event, this led the Australians to create very generous arrangements when they set up their child support system.'

The complexities of other countries' handling of child support were also outlined by another key player. Again the story is one of apparent formulaic superiority over the UK but with less successful enforcement records:

'We are sure that Australia, parts of America and New Zealand have significantly less complicated systems and, therefore, more departures. On this level, these countries appear to be operating better than the UK but it is difficult to make accurate comparisons. We also know that compliance rates vary significantly and are not very good in these other countries. In fact, in some American states the compliance rates are very poor: for example in the southern states of America.'

What problems could have been anticipated and avoided?

Whether or not child support problems were mainly about unpopularity or operational chaos, key players were in several minds about which controversies could and should have been anticipated and possibly avoided. The evidence from interviewees is that some attempt was made to advertise the policy in roadshows headed up by civil servants and politicians. But the media did better than the policy-makers and managed to sell a negative image ahead of the Whitehall caravan. As a key player pointed out, some unpopular policies are more difficult to sell than others:

'We had to sell the poll tax and education reform in the same way. Although no one can believe that we actually made some positive efforts to sell the poll tax. No one can remember anything except its abject unpopularity and failure. We did eventually sell the educational reforms although it did not look like it at the time. These were massively pilloried and had large scale objections but they took hold after a while. The proof of this is that the educational reforms are now being endorsed by the new government. This demonstrates that some policies start off as unpopular and then get accepted. Others stay unpopular and get chucked out. It is difficult to say at the time whether a large unpopularity is a temporary or permanent thing.'

One key player did think that child support policy-makers could have learned at least one lesson from the poll tax struggles:

> 'The poll tax had made civil disobedience acceptable and respectable for the first time in living memory. In fact, civil disobedience is not a very British culture at all. So we started the child support policy with a public that did not think they had to stick with the law at all times.'

Things could also have been learned from the courts about the difficulties inherent in maintenance assessment:

> 'The Lord Chancellor's Department could have advised us just how the British public can frustrate the system by withholding information. This would have helped us anticipate the weight of the problem. I think that after the poll tax we did not fully appreciate how acceptable it had become in the UK for people to withhold information without fear of redress. We also did not learn from the poll tax that people who do not want to pay money, either to local or central government or any authority, will not.'

There was a general feeling amongst those interviewed that whatever progress is made in the craft of policy-making, and however much there are attempts to learn from other policies and other countries' experiences, the concept of child support is, in its own right, problematic. Although the key players interviewed played different roles in the making of the child support policy, there was a high level of agreement on some of the larger issues in child support policy. From the hands-on civil servants and politicians to the lobby groups and scrutineers of government, child support was seen as an inherently difficult policy area but one which, nevertheless, must be pursued. The level of support which the policy has sustained through different governments is an indicator that it will survive its unpopularity. The current intense search for the right formula and the right operational structure bears out the key player hindsight and insight about both the complexity and the importance of this policy. Two final reflections from key players give an insight into some of the unresolved and, possibly unresolvable, problems of child support policy.

> 'I think we would have had cries of protest whatever we had done. There would always have been some sort of inequity – a different sort but nevertheless an inequity of policy. It is in the nature of this kind of policy which involves assessment and a formula for payments and allowances.'

> 'The really big question left for calculations of child support, its operation and its compliance is – how do we calculate guilt and blame and work them into the formula for assessment. These factors were written out of the law so that they could not be used by courts – but that was only in theory. In reality, guilt and blame and all the other emotions still exist in relationship breakdown so there is no reason to suppose that the Child Support Agency can avoid them any more than the courts were able to.'

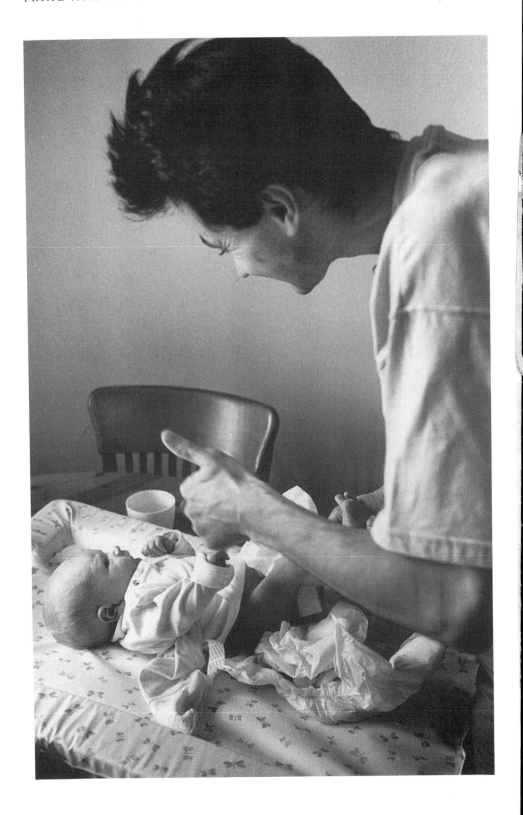

4 Overseas experiences of child support policy

The issue of child support is not, of course, unique to the UK. As divorce rates have grown, and the numbers of children living in lone-parent families has increased, States across the developed world have been forced to confront the problems involved in creating a system for the efficient assessment and collection of child maintenance. Countries have created child support systems which reflect their orientation towards social security and family policy, and in particular the division of financial responsibility for children between their parents and the State.

The experience of other countries can offer valuable lessons to policy-makers grappling with the same problem, although those involved in comparative analysis of welfare policies are becoming increasingly aware of the importance of specifically national elements, and the dangers of an 'off the peg' approach to policy development. In this chapter we aim to do two things:

First, we look at the ways in which overseas experience informed the development of UK child support policy: which countries were examined, the stage of development which their policy had reached at that time, and the analytical framework which was used to select or reject various approaches to child support. This leads us to examine whether the Department of Social Security learnt as much as it could have from the international comparisons it made when the policy was being created.

Secondly, we analyse current child support systems in eight countries, using theoretical models as a framework for understanding contrasting operational features of child support systems such as their scope, determination of amounts due, and methods of enforcement. This section aims to highlight the lessons which can still be drawn from overseas experience; it sets out the range of options which are available in dealing with issues such as second families, shared care and the income of resident parents, but is careful to relate these to their national context.

The development of UK child support policy

In search of a blueprint

This use of comparative policies by the Department of Social Security in the formulation of the UK's child support policy was part of an ongoing, dynamic, process. In concentrating on information which was available at the early stages of policy, our aim is to discover the effects the comparisons had on the early stages of UK child support policy. The Department of Social Security relied mainly on internal sources of information, rather than commissioning an external review. These consisted of a literature

review and visits overseas by Department of Social Security officials. External sources of information, such as submissions by outside agencies such as the Law Society, which referred to overseas experience, were also considered.

The literature review, referred to in *Children Come First* (Department of Social Security, 1990) was a short document which outlined child support systems in the US, Australia, Canada, New Zealand, Sweden, France, and Denmark. According to Department officials this was a background briefing document which did not strongly influence the choice of countries to be studied in more depth. The countries which were selected for closer scrutiny were the USA and Australia which were visited by Department of Social Security officials. This selection was made on the basis of similarity – countries with similar circumstances to the UK, also experiencing difficulties arising from child support. Italy and Spain were not selected, as the nature of family relations and informal family support meant that their situation was not comparable with that of the UK. Germany was considered too different for useful comparisons to be drawn because of its distinctive approach to the financial and legal obligations binding families. Scandinavian countries were also not examined because their welfare provision was seen to have 'adopted an approach which was not proving to be workable for the future' (senior British civil servant). In the USA, Department of Social Security officials chose Wisconsin – seen to be in a different situation to the UK because of the low mobility of its population – and Florida, whose computer system was later used for the UK. New Zealand was also visited by the Department of Social Security at the time it introduced its Back to Work Schemes, although this was at a later date.

At the time when the Department of Social Security looked at the Australian scheme it was being evaluated. Stage 1 had been implemented in June 1988 and consisted of the establishment of the Child Support Agency as part of the Australian Tax Office and with similar enforcement powers (ie. automatic deductions from salaries and wages). The Family Law Amendment 1987, giving courts the power to give priority to children's financial needs, and the Income Test Act for people on benefit were also included in Stage 1. Stage 2, implemented in July 1989, introduced a formula to determine the amount of maintenance the non-custodial parent should pay. The right of appeal continued to operate through the courts.

In the US, child support was determined according to state rules, subject to guidelines set out by the Federal Government. Interest focused on the Wisconsin system which was seen as unique in an American context, and similar to the European advance maintenance systems. A pilot scheme was in place which provided a guaranteed level of maintenance to resident parents where non-resident parents were on a low income.

A missed opportunity?

As discussed above the Department of Social Security concentrated mainly on other English-speaking countries in its search for lessons from abroad. The basis for selecting the countries analysed appears to have been informal and unsystematic. A more

systematic comparison might have been valuable. Although academics were approached to prepare a cross-national study of child support systems, this was ultimately not funded.*

Two main models were in operation, the tax model and the benefit model. Under the tax model used in Australia, the net income of the non-resident parent was calculated and percentage guidelines were used to determine the amount due. This was considered to be a straightforward and simple system but did not resolve the difficulties of trying to track down undeclared income. The benefit model (used in some US states) required two assessments to be made, one of the needs of the non-resident parent, the other of the requirements of the child. This system was perceived as being fairer but more complicated, especially if second families were involved. The Department of Social Security also looked at which departments or bodies were administering child support in other countries. The options from overseas were whether to have a social security-based system as in Wisconsin and Florida or an Inland Revenue-based system as in Australia.

According to the Social Security Select Committee the information collected from the countries selected was sparse. The SSSC had asked the Department of Social Security 'for a note about the effectiveness of child support schemes in Australia and the United States and received some information about the Australian system and limited information about the system operating in Wisconsin'. The information received about Australia was limited to an evaluation of stage 1 (improving collection and enforcement of existing maintenance orders). Stage 2 had not yet been evaluated. As for the Wisconsin scheme 'there is no information about the impact of the formula on the levels of payment ordered and details are vague on the effects of improved collection methods on the amount of maintenance received.' (SSSC, Third Report, 1990-1, Evidence, p29).

In their analysis of the Australian and American systems, British policy-makers seem to have concentrated on specific questions relating to the operation of the system without looking to the broader context of child support policies generally. The purpose of the analysis appears to have been tightly focused on finding the most effective and fair way of getting non-resident parents to pay for their children. Yet underlying the narrow remit of this question is the wider context of policies affecting resident parents, non-resident parents, and children, which needs to be considered to achieve cohesiveness and efficiency in the policy formulated.

The Department of Social Security placed a high value on fairness, opting for the benefit model for evaluating child support because it was seen as fairer, although it was more complicated to administer. Yet, for reasons which were not made clear, it opted for a retrospective policy, when both Australia and the USA had rejected this approach because of the opposition revealed by public consultation.

---

*A comparison of child support systems in ten European countries has subsequently been undertaken by York University (Corden, forthcoming).

Lessons for the future?

There may be valuable lessons which can still be learnt from looking at how other countries deal with child support, but in order to make valid comparisons it is necessary to take account of the full range of cultural, social, demographic, and economic factors which exists.

At the level of theoretical analysis, child support systems can also be classified on the basis of their guiding principles. These principles may, in turn, influence the details of policy, and affect the range of options seen to be available in a given country.

Millar (1996) draws on the literature of comparative welfare state policy (see, for example, Esping-Andersen, 1990), to contrast an 'Anglo-Saxon' model, adopted by the USA, Australia, Canada and New Zealand, as well as the USA, where the State intervenes to reinforce private family obligations, with a 'Scandinavian' model, found in Norway, Sweden, Germany and France, where the State guarantees or advances maintenance in case of default. The Anglo-Saxon model is dependent on effective enforcement, and the financial capacity of the non-resident parent, whereas the Scandinavian model relies on the level of state resources it is able to command. However, as child support involves not only welfare provision, but systems of family law, this classification may obscure important dimensions of difference. For instance, Norway, Sweden, France and Germany, grouped together in this model, have very different traditions of family law.

Ergas (1990) avoids such complications by distinguishing child support systems solely by reference to the degree of responsibility assigned to the individual or the state. He describes a model of maximum public responsibility where public institutions assume responsibility for child care and the participation of women in the labour market. Service delivery operates on a universal basis, rather than being subsidised or selective. The broad outlines of policies, and the resources to support them, are provided by central government, but administration takes place at a local level. By contrast, under the model of maximum private responsibility, childcare, family organisation and the employment of women are viewed as private matters. The fundamental aim of public intervention is to provide a safety net in cases of hardship. Central control of policy is reduced, and responsibility is divided between private actors, local government and third sector organisations. This model, unlike Millar's, would group Germany with the USA, whereas, as we shall see, many features of their child support systems stand in sharp contrast to each other.

A third model is offered by Lefaucheur (1997), based not on contemporary principles underlying child support, but on historical concerns about population and morality in each country at different periods. For our purposes, this model is particularly useful in highlighting distinctions between English-speaking countries, which are often regarded as similar by policy analysts, and appear to have been a focus for those creating the UK child support policy for this reason. Thus Lefaucheur's model would distinguish between the UK, where policy has historically emphasised the Christian duty of the community to provide support for fatherless children, and the USA, where a continuing emphasis on the establishment of paternity can be traced to 'Malthusian' concerns about population control in the past.

In moving on to compare practical features of child support systems in the countries selected, our aim is to clarify the analytical process by relating practice to underlying assumptions which often remain implicit. Child support systems are compared on key components in order to present an overview of the range of options available. This comparison is necessarily schematic, and this should be borne in mind when evaluating the success of child support systems in individual countries, and, in particular, in assessing the usefulness or transferability of specific elements of a system. Readers requiring more information on maintenance regimes in European countries should refer to Corden (forthcoming). References to material for the USA and Australia are provided in the bibliography.

Transferability is an issue with all comparative policy-making, and, as Castles (1993) has argued, it is particularly so with policies involving implicit or culturally specific values. As practice has shown, child support is an extremely sensitive and personal area where policy-makers need to tread carefully. A multitude of factors come into play which need to be considered if best practice from overseas is to be applied in the UK. These are:

- **composition of lone-parent population:** demography (marital status, age, qualifications), employment rates (including an interface with benefit levels and childcare provision);
- **characteristics of non-resident parents:** income distribution, geographical mobility, income mobility, levels of self employment;
- **values:** responsibility for children as part of the right to be a parent; gender responsibility for sexual behaviour (in Austria and Scandinavian countries, for example, sympathy does not lie with the man pursued for child support after a casual relationship by a woman who 'got herself pregnant', the man is considered foolish to have put himself in that situation initially).

These variables affect the operation of policies in practice and need to be considered when examining the possibilities of transferring policies from one system into another.

A total of eight countries were compared during this review. Information was collated from a variety of published sources, and supplementary data was provided by national experts, including officials and academic commentators. The countries were Norway, Sweden, France, Germany, Austria, the Netherlands, the USA, and Australia. Norway and Sweden were chosen as examples of Scandinavian welfare states also experiencing the consequences of a high proportion of births outside marriage. France, Germany, Austria and the Netherlands were selected as examples of other European countries at similar stages of economic development to the UK, and with similar proportions of lone-parent families. In the case of Germany and Austria, there had also been recent reforms of the child support system. Finally, the USA and Australia were chosen for their similar Anglo-Saxon culture, and because they were examined by the Department of Social Security. Choosing these countries again makes it possible to place them in a wider context, enabling us to measure the relative value of concentrating exclusively on these Anglo-Saxon countries. Spain, Italy, and Greece were not included in our study because of their very different proportions of lone-parent families, welfare systems and

Table 4.1	**Demographic indicators relevant to child support**					
	Lone parents as percentage of all households with children	Marriage rate per 1,000	Divorce rate per 1,000	Percentage of births to unmarried women	Mean age of women at first marriage	Teen births per 1,000
Norway	20.6	4.6	2.5	43	26.2	17
Sweden	18.0	3.9	2.5	50	27.6	13
Australia	17.8	6.2	2.7	24	-	22
Germany	19.0	5.4	2.0	15	25.9	9
					23.7*	44*
Austria	15.3	5.4	2.1	25	25.7	23
France	13.2	4.4	2.0	32	26.1	9
USA	28.9	9.1	4.6	28	23.0	78
Netherlands	15.9	5.4	2.4	13	25.9	8
United Kingdom	20.9	5.9	3.1	31	25.2	33

* former East Germany

Sources:
Column 1: Bradshaw et al., 1996, (Table 2.3; data circa 1992)
Columns 2 and 3: UN, 1997 (Tables 23 and 25; data circa 1994)
Columns 4 to 6: UN, 1998 (Tables 6 and 23; data circa 1990)

stages of economic development. Table 4.1 presents summary information on the demographic situation in the countries compared in this chapter. Information specific to each of the eight countries is contained in the boxes at the end of this chapter.

Comparing components of child support

The sections below compare five key features of child support systems across the countries in the study, and aim to highlight the range of options available. Given the number of countries covered, and the variety of alternatives available, they cannot aim to be fully comprehensive; what they do provide is a sense of how different countries have resolved issues such as the methods for calculating child support, the choice of administrative mechanisms, and the means of enforcing child support payments. The use of a child support system is generally optional for parents who are not on benefit but those claiming social assistance are usually required to co-operate with child support procedures, although most countries have some procedures for exempting those in difficult circumstances, particularly domestic violence.

Determining liability and agreeing payment

In the case of children born outside marriage it is necessary to establish paternity for a financial obligation to arise. The concept of illegitimacy has been abandoned in all of the eight countries examined. This happened first in Norway and Sweden, with Germany, Austria and the Netherlands harmonising the situation between children born in and out of marriage over the last two to three years. There is now only one set of legal rules concerning child support, providing that where the mother is not married no support is claimed from the father before paternity has been established (by voluntary recognition or the courts). In most countries in the review paternity is established by the father's acknowledgement or on the mother's declaration, and is satisfied via biological rather than social paternity. Different approaches have been used to simplify the identification of fathers of children born outside marriage, with active encouragement to register paternity at the hospital in the US, simplified administrative procedures and financial incentives.

The main options for formalising child support are private agreements, arrangements set by the courts or administratively-settled arrangements. These arrangements can work independently or in combination, as in most countries. Private agreements about child support are common throughout Europe, but often their legal scope and practical importance are uncertain. Overall, support agreements can be made without official consent and without the observance of any particular form. This is the accepted rule in Norway and Sweden. However controls are available after the making of the contract to ensure the support claims of children cannot be waived or to allow for an agreement to be revised. In Norway, the rule is that parents cannot contract for less than the minimum which would eventually be paid from public funds. In Sweden, an agreement can be amended by the courts if it is 'unreasonable' and in the Netherlands if brought about 'with gross misunderstanding of the legal yardsticks'. In a few countries, such as France and Austria, private agreements are only valid if official consent is granted, as in the case of support agreements made in the context of divorce by mutual consent. In these cases the judge will only approve of arrangements compatible with the interests of the child.

A fully court-based system is one where courts are responsible for assessing liability for child support payments, setting amounts due and enforcing payment. This is the system in place in Germany and Austria. Courts can also operate as a residual system, as in the UK and the US, or as an appeals system as in Australia. In an administrative system, the transfer of monies from the non-resident parent to the resident parent is arranged either through a child support agency (as in the UK and Australia) or by the municipal authorities (as in most other countries examined in this study). This system can be full, handling child support claims against all non-resident parents as in Australia, or residual, collecting from the non-resident parent only where the resident parent is on benefit. The latter is not an explicit objective of policy in any country, but is a frequent outcome, where resources are focused on this group as in many USA states.

Continuity in the application of guidelines through the judicial and administrative systems is essential. Experience in the US shows that assessments set by the courts below guidelines account for a significant loss in the amounts of child support collected nationally. Another problem arising from court-based systems is the under-estimation of income, particularly among self-employed non-resident parents. Some countries, such as France, have limited this to an extent by using gross income rather than net income as the base for the calculation.

The amount of child support

When considering the levels at which support is set, it is important also to take into account any underlying assumptions that may exist, ie. that the resident parent is in paid employment, as in France, or that the rights of the child are to be paramount, as in Austria.

In setting amounts of child support there are two main types of system: basic support and a quota system.

- **The basic support or minimum standard system**
  This corresponds to sums of money seen as necessary or at least desirable for every child, and is found in the German system of *Regelunterhalt* for the first six years of a child's life, the Dutch system of social minimum, *AlgemenebijstandsWet*, which is linked to the minimum wage and indexed, and the French system of *Allocation de Soutien Familial* until the youngest child is three years old. Basic support may also be linked to support tables with scales of increasing, fixed, amounts to be paid by parents in different income groups which ensure that the child obtains at least a certain minimum, and ultimately a fair share, of the non-resident parent's income. These are mostly used in Germany, where quite a few courts have elaborated their own tables and guidelines, although by far the most used are the Dusseldorf tables.
- **The quota or percentage system**
  This is based on receiving a definite proportion of the non-resident parent's net income, and may be calculated according to the number of children, as in Norway and Australia, or also include the age of the children, as in Sweden and Austria.

Both these systems can be used in one of three ways: by applying a formula, or using guidelines, or according to certain principles weighed up by the courts on a discretionary, case by case, basis. Broadly speaking a formula or guidelines can be set out according to the following principles:

- **cost sharing,** which calculates the cost of rearing a child and then allocates that cost between the parents;
- **income sharing,** where a certain percentage of parental income is allocated to the support of children; or
- **income equalisation,** where the income of first and second households is pooled and apportioned according to the size and composition of each household.

There are also a number of general criteria to be taken into account when assessing child support. In determining the amounts of child support to be paid by a non-resident parent, the needs of the child and the means of the parent are considered. But the weight attributed to these varies from country to country, and even within countries. Some of the measures used are:

- the means of the parent
- the needs of the child,
- the standard of living of the family.

The means of the parent is the only test mentioned in France and the Netherlands. In most European countries officially fixed support payments vary greatly according to means. If the non-resident parent has established a second family the European norm is that the needs of all the children are considered on an equal footing. This may result in both families receiving benefits if their income falls below a certain level. Whether or not the resident parent's earning capacity should be taken into account has not generally been given much consideration in child support systems in Europe, although it is considered in the benefit systems. In Austria the resident parent is deemed to have fulfilled his or her duty by personal care for the child but must also make a financial contribution 'in so far as the other parent is incapable of covering all the needs of the child or would have to pay more than is appropriate to his station in life'.

A test based on the 'needs of the child' is never referred to on its own, partly because the usefulness of this test is limited by frequent lack of means, but also because it is very difficult to define 'normal' or 'reasonable' living expenses at higher income levels without reference to some external standards. More commonly used is the individual standard of living previously enjoyed by the complete family or at present by the better-situated parent. This measure is used in France ('children should neither lose nor gain by their parents' divorce') and in many other European countries.

Most countries examined in this report do not require unemployed non-resident parents or non-resident parents on a very low income to pay child support. In Australia and some US states all non-resident parents are required to pay a minimum amount regardless of financial circumstances. The argument is that lack of money should not be a bar to exercising responsibility for children. A countervailing view is that transferring money from one person on benefits to another recipient of benefits amounts to 'churning' and is of little real value, and indeed, incurs costs which are inefficent.

Great divergence exists between countries on when the obligation should end. It is generally agreed that people over the age of majority can finance their higher studies themselves. In Austria the law simply says that parental support duty continues until the child becomes self-supporting, without any reference to majority.

Guaranteed payments

In the case of non-payment or delayed payment all the countries examined offer some protection. This is either in the form of basic social assistance as in the Netherlands, Australia and the US, or advance payment of sums due as in France, Germany, Austria, Norway and Sweden. In the latter case, a public authority, often the social security office, guarantees a specified level of child support by advancing support payments to the resident parent if payment by the non-resident parent is not made or is irregular. In addition, the same or another agency assumes responsibility for the collection of child support from the absent parent, crediting what is collected against the payments advanced. Within this framework, policies vary across countries depending on whether the public authority acts for all resident parents or only resident parents on low incomes, whether a court order is necessary for the process to be initiated, whether the support is for the mother and child or only for the child, and whether the primary concern is with reducing the burden on the State or ensuring adequate support for the child.

The countries providing a guarantee system fall into two categories: countries that guarantee child support in the form of a benefit with conditions attached, as in France (around £47.00 per month, providing the resident parent is not cohabiting) and Germany (£116.00 per month for children under 13 years old, payable for a maximum of six years) and those that guarantee support without conditions as in Sweden (around £80.00 per month) and in Norway (around £70.00 per month). Some countries (such as Sweden) provide indefinite guarantees, whilst others (such as Germany and France) have time limits for this type of support.

Updating mechanisms

For basic support, uprating can be carried out in line with the official consumer price index. Germany, for fear of stimulating inflation, used to set new levels of *Regelunterhalt* at discretionary periods (usually every two to three years), but from 1998 will update every two years in line with the index used for pension rates. Statutory indexation clauses are used in the Netherlands, Sweden, and Norway. This offers inbuilt protection from the effects of inflation to resident parents, and relieves the courts and other authorities from petitions for individual amendment of support award. However the net income of many non-resident parents does not necessarily increase at the same pace. Finally, judicial indexation clauses are used in France. A wide variety of indexes relating to costs or wages is used although a 5 per cent variation is the most common measure required. If the indexation is dependent on the discretion of the courts, rather than statutory, the risk of undue hardship for the non-resident parent is reduced but uncertainties and errors increase.

As well as updating child support to protect its value in real terms, there are also measures to take into account changes in the circumstances of parents – both resident and non-resident parent. The changes taken into account vary between countries, as does the manner in which they are included (through the courts, or administratively). There are, however, some core changes, such as income and employment, which are considered in all the countries examined. Changes in circumstances affect not only the support payable by the non-resident parent but also how much state assistance the resident parent receives to pursue maintenance from the non-resident parent. Generally, where state assistance is focused on resident parents on benefits, it reduces or stops when the resident parent enters paid employment.

Methods of enforcement

These can be direct (attachment of earnings or pay) or indirect (sanctions for non-support). Increasingly, European countries are favouring direct enforcement rather than sanctions (Corden, forthcoming). Enforcement can be through special collection agencies, that is public authorities acting as special collection agencies for child support either at their own behest or at the request of the resident parent. These agencies can also act independently, as in the Netherlands and Germany, or in co-ordination with systems connected with advance support, as in Norway and Sweden, where recovery of public advance support is fixed at a specified level, even if higher amounts have been assessed as due to the child. The State will seek reimbursement from the non-resident parent and leave the claim for any surplus amount to be pursued by the resident parent.

In some countries, as in the US state of Wisconsin, the collection of even nominal amounts from the unemployed and pensioners is seen as a point of principle, a means of making non-resident parents aware of their responsibilities towards their children. Under recent Federal legislation (Personal Responsibility and Work Opportunity Act, 1996) each state must operate a Child Support Enforcement Programme meeting Federal requirements in order to be eligible for Temporary Assistance to Needy Families block grants. The new provisions include: national new hire reporting system, streamlined paternity establishment, uniform inter-state child support laws, computerised state-wide collections, new penalties (revoking drivers and professional licences, seizing assets and community service, as well as deductions from earnings), and grants to programmes improving the access and visitation rights of non-resident parents.

No easy answers

The evidence reviewed in this chapter appears to suggest some convergence in the administration of child support policy, alongside a great deal of diversity in the content of policy. The streamlining of procedures for children born to married and unmarried parents, the use of centralised child support agencies to collect, if not assess, maintenance, and an increasing emphasis on direct enforcement of child support obligations through the wage packet can be seen in most of the countries examined. Different child support systems have evolved not only to meet needs created by contrasting demographic, social and economic situations, but to give expression to differing norms in respect of family life and the role of the State. Thus advance payments of maintenance are more characteristic of states which theoretical models would classify as 'Scandinavian' or favouring 'maximum public responsibility', whilst requiring minimum payments even of those on very low incomes is a response typical of a 'Liberal' or 'maximum private responsibility' state. However, many other aspects of child support, such as the rationale for determining the amount due or the treatment of the resident parent's earnings are less easy to classify, and it is arguable that none of the theoretical models presented adequately captures the complexity involved. As far as UK policy is concerned, we should perhaps look for lessons not in the details of the policies adopted in other countries, which have, after all, been designed to meet different needs, but in the ways in which policy questions have been framed, and the issues which have surfaced during public debate.

Country profile: Australia

Demography*

Lone-parent families account for around one in six households with children in Australia. Australia is similar to the UK in having a high marriage and divorce rate. Around a quarter of births are to unmarried women; this places it in the middle rank, below the USA and the UK, but higher than any other Western European country except Austria. Rates of teenage birth are also similar to Austria, at 22 per thousand.

Provision for lone parents

The main benefit for lone parents in Australia is Parental Allowance, which pays a basic amount to any lone parent with at least one child under 16. It is set at the same level as the old-age pension, with extra entitlements for children. Help with housing costs, medical and pharmaceutical costs may also be available. About 72% of lone parents receive this benefit and up to 22% of those on benefit also have some earnings. Somewhat over 40% of lone mothers overall are employed. Everyone claiming Parental Allowance is required to take action to obtain child support. The JET (Jobs, Education and Training) scheme introduced in 1989 helps lone parents with education and training, finding work, and childcare placements.

Calculation of child support

The Child Support Act was passed in 1988 with the aim of increasing maintenance payments, as part of a wider package of schemes directed at lone-parent families which were themselves part of a wider review of the nature and structure of social security benefits.

The system evolved gradually over a period: although the idea of an Agency was first mooted in 1980, this did not come into force until 1988. Following extensive public consultation, it was decided that the scheme should not be retrospective and that it would be introduced in two stages, the first involving the enforcement of existing maintenance (from 1988) whilst the involvement of the Agency in assessing maintenance did not begin until 1989.

Maintenance is assessed as a percentage of taxable income, net of standard deductions (based on benefit levels) for the non-resident parent and any partner or children in the household. The percentages are:

- *18% for 1 child*
- *27% for 2 children*
- *32% for 3 children*
- *34% for 4 children*
- *36% for 5 or more children*

The Agency uses a variant of the formula to deal with the situation of divided custody (where each parent has resident children of the relationship) and shared custody (where a child spends roughly equal amounts of time with each parent she or he is counted as 0.5). Hence the percentages are as follows:

*see Table 4.1 p.40

- *12% for 0.5 children*
- *18% for 1 child*
- *24% for 1.5 children*
- *27% for 2 children*
- *30% for 2.5 children*

and so on, rising to a maximum of 36 per cent for five or more children. A maintenance bill is worked out for each parent, and the one with the highest bill pays the amount of the difference to the other parent. Significant amounts are therefore payable only if there are large disparities in taxable income.

There is a total disregard of maintenance up to £1,700 per year for a lone parent and one child, with around £500 extra per child per year. Above this level there is a 50% taper for benefits.

Minimum amount

Since 1997 the non-resident parent is required to pay a minimum payment of £10 per week, regardless of their financial circumstances.

Guaranteed payments

There is no guaranteed maintenance in Australia.

Current issues

Following an Inquiry in late 1993, set up as a direct result of the numbers of complaints made to the Ombudsman and to senators and MPs, which made over 150 recommendations for the future development of child support policy, changes have been introduced. From 1997, all non-resident parents are required to pay a minimum amount of maintenance. Some loopholes which allowed the manipulation of taxable income to reduce liability have been closed. Liability is reduced where the non-resident parent has a second family or where the resident parent is earning significantly more than average wages. Average levels of maintenance have increased, and the Agency enjoys a 2/3 compliance rate. Parents are encouraged (and even required) to move off the scheme once payment has become reliable.

The Inquiry received over 6,000 submissions (the largest ever received by a Parliamentary Inquiry in Australia): a quarter of all submissions argued that the formula was too harsh. However, not everyone is convinced of the need for reform. A dissenting report was presented to the Inquiry by Senator Belinda Neal, who argued for the extension of child support legislation to those currently excluded from its scope, and against the capping of non-resident parents' assessable incomes and the reduction of the custodial parent's disregard. It has been argued that these changes, in response to lobbying on behalf of non-resident parents, seriously undermine the original intentions of the scheme. It is argued that by responding to the 'squeaky wheels' of people who complain, instead of satisfied customers, policy-makers may be neglecting the real needs of children.

Country profile: Austria

Demography

Almost one in seven families with children in Austria is headed by a lone parent. The marriage rate is similar to that in the UK, but the divorce rate is lower; women also marry younger in Austria than in most of the other countries studied. Around a quarter of all births are to unmarried women, and the teenage birth rate is fairly high; only the UK and the USA have higher rates.

Provision for lone parents

Lone parents receive a tax allowance of £240 in addition to the single person's allowance of £240 per year. Child tax allowances (for all families) amount to £34 per child per month. Lone parents are more likely than their married counterparts to be in work: those receiving social assistance are obliged to seek work once their youngest child is three.

Calculation of child support

Parents have a duty under Austrian constitutional law to pay maintenance for any child, whether born inside or outside marriage, in accordance with the child's needs and their standard of living. The paternity of children born outside marriage is established by judgment or acknowledgement. The resident parent's contribution is deemed to be met (partially or in total) by the work which they carry out in caring for the child. The duty to pay maintenance continues until the age of 28 in cases where the young person is still undergoing education or professional training. Where it is impossible for parents to fulfil their obligations, grandparents may be called upon to pay maintenance, provided that to do so would not jeopardise their own livelihood.

Maintenance is determined in non-litigious proceedings. To avoid this lengthy procedure there are summary proceedings which fix a preliminary maintenance which ensures a basic living standard for the child. Enforcement is through the bailiff. The child's legal representative may entrust the youth welfare officer with a mandate to determine and enforce the child's claims. The child support system was set up in 1970, and revised in 1980. Court guidelines specify the following percentages of the non-resident parent's net average monthly earnings, depending on the age of the child:

- *16% aged 0-5*
- *18% aged 6-10*
- *20% aged 11-15*
- *22% aged 15+*

Where there is responsibility for several children, or for a non-working spouse, the percentages are reduced accordingly, usually by 2 to 3 per cent.

Failure to pay maintenance can lead to criminal proceedings by the state.

Minimum amount

Non-resident parents are not required to pay a minimum amount. Unemployed people and those on very low incomes are not obliged to pay maintenance.

Guaranteed payments

There is an advance maintenance system, in place since 1976, available for minor children where the absent parent is no longer living with the child and has not met his/her legal obligations. The State will also make advance payment where the liable parent cannot be found or is serving a prison sentence for more than one month. Eligibility for advance payments for child support is not means-tested.

Claims must be based on a legal order, that is a court decision setting the amount of child support, or an out-of-court agreement, subsequently approved by the court. An attempt to collect the child support by means of an income execution must have failed in the six months prior to the application for advance payment. The amount of the advance depends on the amount of child support set in court order, although there is an upper limit.

Advance payments are granted for a period of not more than three years. Renewals can be granted for three years. Advance payments are raised or reduced if the amount of mainte-nance is raised or reduced. They are only paid for minors. No advances are payable in situations where it is obvious that the debtor is in no position to pay support (either because of sickness or inability to earn an income).

The costs of this scheme amounted to around ATS 1 billion in 1997; only slightly more than 40 per cent of overall costs were recovered from liable parents. Recovery from wage-dependent people or employees is very effective (around 90%), but it is not so effective from self-employed people, who even the Inland Revenue have difficulty tracking down. There are also difficulties with payments from unemployed people who are not obliged to pay maintenance.

Current issues

The courts have recently ruled that maintenance should be tax deductible for the non-resident parent, in accordance with established guidelines on the costs of children. There are no plans for reform of child support nor any manifestations of dissatisfaction with the current system, although there is a persistent problem of lone parents living on low incomes.

Country profile: France

Demography

Lone-parent families account for around one in eight families with children in France. France has a low marriage rate and a low divorce rate. Almost a third of births are to unmarried women, but the rate of teenage birth is very low at only nine per thousand.

Provision for lone parents

There are two main benefits for lone parents, *Allocation Soutien Familial (ASF)*, a non-contributory benefit for families where there is no second parent; and *Allocation de Parent Isole (API)* a means-tested and more generous alternative to *Revenue Minimum D'Insertion (RMI)*, the general social assistance benefit, it is payable for 12 months after divorce or separation or until the youngest child is three years old. When API eligibility ceases the lone parent may claim RMI, which involves making a *contrat d'insertion* (which may include participation in a job creation or training programme). Most lone parents are in employment, but they have been disproportionately affected by recent rises in unemployment.

When a child is born in France the father does not have to be named, and where this is the case there is no obligation to maintain, and entitlement to ASF follows. Where there is a recognised father, he has an obligation to maintain which if not met gives rise to ASF.

Calculation of child support

In the case of divorcing parents the judge will set the amount of child support along with the right to visit. Child support agreements are required by the judge when the divorce is by mutual consent and joint petition (over 40 per cent of divorces). Cohabiting couples can also use the courts to decide on the amount of child support where they are unable to agree arrangements on separation.

In both cases the judge estimates the amount of child support freely, taking into account the needs of the children and the income of the non-resident parent, but there are no formal guidelines and the amounts awarded are generally low. They range from around £40 per child per month to £800 per child per month; £80 per child per month is an average level. Child support is only awarded in about two out of three cases.

Enforcement

Child support is not paid in about one in ten cases and irregularly paid in about 40 per cent of cases. The resident parent can ask the family benefits office to recover the child support debt on his or her behalf after two months of non-payment. Payments can be deducted from the salary or bank account of the non-resident parent, or collected by a tax collector or bailiff.

Minimum amount

There is provision to recover a minimum amount of maintenance (around £60 per month as at 1 January 1995) but it is rarely used.

Guaranteed payments

If the resident parent is not married or cohabiting they can receive family support benefit (*Allocation de Soutien Familial (ASF)* of £47 per month per child in 1998) as an advance on unpaid child support. In 60% to 70% of cases the *Caisse Allocations Familiales (CAF)* consider that the amount is not actually recoverable, but CAF will continue to pay ASF to lone parents provided that they are on their own, ie. do not remarry or cohabit. In all cases of doubt the benefit is not payable. By June 1997 there were 484,600 recipients, almost all of them women.

Country profile: Germany

Demography

Almost one in five households with children in Germany is headed by a lone parent. Germany has a high marriage rate and a fairly low divorce rate; only 15 per cent of births are to unmarried women. Women marry later in West Germany than in the former GDR, and teenage births are very much higher, at 44 per thousand, in the former GDR than in the old *Länder*.

Provision for lone parents

There is no special provision for lone parents in Germany. Lone parents have fairly low rates of employment, especially when their children are young, but only around 10% are in receipt of social assistance. Maintenance payments appear to be an important source of income for lone parents.

Calculation of child support

All non-resident parents are obliged to pay child support. The resident parent is viewed as having fulfilled their obligation in kind in the form of care, provision and accommodation. The statutory rule that child support should be granted according to the parents' 'station in life' is now interpreted by reference to the child's needs and the parents' financial ability. This has led to the development of 'support tables' used by the courts, the most famous of which are the 'Dusseldorf tables' which calculate a fixed amount according to the monthly net income of the non-resident parent and the age of the child. There is an overall limit to liability at each income level which is set at around 2.5 times the for a level a young person aged 18 or more. These are used as guidelines rather than rigid requirements. The amounts due are set at the minimum (see below) for incomes below £800 per month, and increase in line with income up to £2,667 per month. The amounts for this highest income level are:

- *£222 per child under 7 years*
- *£268 per child aged 7-12*
- *£315 per child aged 13-18*
- *£362 per child (over 18 years)*

Above this, no guidelines are suggested and child support is assumed to be negotiated.

Minimum amount

The minimum amount was established in 1969 for children born out of wedlock. It is calculated on the basis of the needs of a child cared for by the mother at what is generally regarded as a very modest living standard. The amount is fixed independently of the non-resident parent's income at three different levels according to the age of the child. From 1 July 1998, these are:

- *£116 per child aged under 7 years (£115 in former East)*
- *£140 per child aged 7-12 (£127 in former East)*
- *£167 per child aged 13-18 (£150 in former East)*

These amounts had previously been uprated irregularly, but are now to be uprated every two years in line with the index used for pension rates. Child allowances are deducted from the amount. Minimum amounts can be enforced through a simplified procedure, which eliminated lengthy investigations into the income of the non-resident parent.

Guaranteed payments

A system for the advance payment of maintenance (*Unterhaltvorschuss*) was set up in 1979. Payments can be made for children under the age of 13, for a maximum of six years. The amounts of the advance payment are based on the minimum child support amounts for children born outside marriage, but they are also available to all children with a non-resident parent who is not paying maintenance. The *Land* decides which organisation should administer it (usually the Office of Child and Youth Welfare). The costs of this measure are shared equally between the Federal State and the *Länder*.

Enforcement

Action is taken to collect maintenance from liable parents, but the recovery rate is poor, at around only 15 per cent. Responsibility for enforcement has been devolved to the district and municipal authorities in most *Länder*.

Current issues

There have been recent reforms of the German maintenance system, which have extended the administrative procedure which had been developed for children born outside marriage and made it available to divorcing couples as an alternative to legal proceedings, which are slower and more costly. Those who wish to do so, usually in cases where the non-resident parent has a high income, are still entitled to seek higher amounts of maintenance through the courts.

For payments set at anything up to 1.5 times the minimum amount, the order can be made by a court officer, and no evidence of income need be supplied if there is no dispute between the parents. If the non-resident parent disputes the amount, litigation is necessary. Claims for maintenance at a rate higher than 1.5 times the compulsory minimum involve legal action. In divorce cases, this will be dealt with as part of the overall divorce procedure. Subsequent changes (eg. because of income changes) can be made under the simplified procedure by a court official.

Country profile: The Netherlands

Demography

Around 16 per cent of families with children in the Netherlands are headed by a lone parent; this is in the lower range for the countries in this study. The Netherlands has a high marriage rate and a divorce rate in the middle range. Only 13 per cent of births are to unmarried mothers, and the rate of teenage births is the lowest of all the countries studied.

Provision for lone parents

There are no special benefits for lone parents, other than those paid as incentives to return to work. Lone parents do not have to be available for work while they have a child under the age of five. Social assistance (which can include help with mortgage interest payments) is provided by the municipality under the General Assistance Act, until recently at the level of 90 per cent of the minimum wage, and is largely financed by central government. It can be paid as a supplement to low earnings for up to two years, at the discretion of the municipality. Around two-thirds of lone mothers receive social assistance. In a context of low rates of single parenthood and low female labour force participation, policy in the Netherlands has been characterised by its readiness to guarantee public income rather than compel mothers of young children to work. This may change with increasing pressures for cutbacks in welfare. As from January 1996, changes in the structure of benefit rates mean that central government will only pay 70 per cent of the minimum wage for lone parents, and the remaining 20 per cent will only be paid if the claimant can prove his or her costs are not shared with anyone else.

Calculation of child support

The father of a child both inside or outside marriage is legally obliged to support his child. Parents are encouraged to reach voluntary arrangements for child support. Where they are unable to agree, amounts of child support can be decided by the District Court. They do this using a set of tables, known as the TREMA tables, which contain complex formulae for the assessment of maintenance. A number of factors are taken into account in assessing the capacity to pay of both the resident and non-resident parent:

- assessable income is calculated by deducting amounts for living expenses, which are based on social assistance rates, from gross income;

- for the non-resident parent allowance is made for the costs of setting up a new home and the costs of contact with the children;

- where the non-resident parent has a second family, assessable income is reduced by around 50 per cent to reflect an explicit principle that people should be free to form new relationships;

- partners of non-resident parents are expected to contribute to the maintenance of their own natural children, whether living with them or elsewhere, and may also be assessed as partially liable for their partner's children if their relationship is in effect that of a parent;

- where the resident parent has entered a new relationship, the decision about liability for maintenance between a step-parent and a non-resident parent is based on an assessment of the relationship between the child and the non-resident parent, including such issues as whose surname the child bears and how frequently contact occurs.

Because of all the complex factors which are taken into account, it is difficult to provide an illustrative example, however, £78 per child per month is a typical amount of maintenance.

Where a lone parent claims means-tested benefits, voluntary payments which are too low may be overturned and replaced with a payment calculated by the National Bureau for the Recovery of Child Maintenance (known as the LBIO), again based on the TREMA tables. Decisions made by the District Court, however, will not be altered.

Enforcement

Automatic payment (standing orders) are usually made from the bank (and set up as part of divorce proceedings). A Central Registration for citizens makes it possible to trace absent fathers, because as soon as someone appears in a municipal registry that person also appears on the central system. Levels of compliance with the new arrangements are described as good, and do not appear to vary significantly according to whether the parents were married, although there is no published quantitative data as yet.

Where maintenance payments have been missed at least once in the previous six months, or where the parents request this service, maintenance can be collected by LBIO. This agency was created as part of the child support reforms in 1993; maintenance had previously been collected by the 19 local offices of the child welfare office. Non-resident parents are charged a collection fee equal to ten per cent of their assessed child support liability, as an incentive to make private arrangements.

Minimum amount

There is no set minimum amount which must be paid by a non-resident parent.

Guaranteed payments

There is no system of advance maintenance in the Netherlands. Means-tested benefits are the only type of replacement income for a lone parent who does not receive maintenance.

Current issues

The child support system which is now in place was introduced because so few non-resident parents were paying maintenance and because resident parents were not taking action to secure maintenance. It is generally regarded as effective, and appears to have generated very little debate, although as it has only been fully operational since January 1997, it may be too early to judge.

Country profile: Norway

Demography

Lone-parent families account for around one in five families with children in Norway. Norway has a low marriage rate and a divorce rate in the middle range. Over 40 per cent of births are to unmarried women, but most are not to very young women: the rate of teenage births is 17 per thousand, above that for Sweden, France and the Netherlands, but below the other countries in the study.

Provision for lone parents

Lone parents receive additional child benefit (as if they had one extra child) and also have special tax allowances. Approximately two-thirds of lone parents in Norway are in paid employment; many work part-time. Lone parents who are unable to work because of childcare problems are entitled to receive Transitional Benefit; around a third also claim social assistance in addition to Transitional Benefit. Claimants of Transitional Benefit are required to use the Maintenance Contribution Collection Agency. Transitional Benefit can be paid for a maximum of three years (or five years if the resident parent is in full-time education); before 1998 it was available to any lone parent with a child aged under ten. Maintenance paid above the level of the advance maintenance payment (see below) is deducted from Transitional Benefit at the rate of 70 per cent (previously 100 per cent).

Calculation of child support

From 1956, there were two systems of child maintenance, for married and unmarried parents. Divorcing parents were dealt with by the courts, whilst unmarried mothers were the responsibility of the local authority. The Children Act of 1981 equalised the position between married and unmarried parents, and brought cases under the jurisdiction of the local authority, although parents could still go to court if they wished. Awards were discretionary, and there were no set guidelines, with the result that the assessment of maintenance often took up to a year. From 1989, set percentages of income have been used.

Parents are free to make voluntary arrangements for child support, provided that the sum agreed is at least the amount of the guaranteed maintenance payment, which in January 1995 was set at around £70 per month. Where the parents cannot reach an agreement, parents can use the Maintenance Contribution Collection Agency; nine out of ten parents use this Agency. Since 1989, child maintenance has been assessed as a simple percentage of the non-resident parent's income:

- *11% for 1 child*
- *18% for 2 children*
- *24% for 3 children*
- *28% for 4 or more children*

The amounts are currently based on the income of the non-resident parent; the income of the resident parent is not taken into account. Where there is a second family the percentages are divided. A parent with one resident and one non-resident child is liable for 9% of income for each. Where the child lives equally with both parents, or where the income of the non-resident parent is very low, these percentages are not applied. Maintenance for those aged 18 or over and still in education is also decided on a discretionary basis. Half of non-resident parents pay maintenance for one child; the average payment of maintenance for one child in 1995 was £94 per month.

Minimum amount

There is no minimum amount which must be paid by all non-resident parents regardless of income.

Guaranteed payments

Unmarried mothers have been guaranteed a minimum level of child support since the 1950s. Advance payments of maintenance have been available to all lone parents since 1989. The amount was around £70 per month as at January 1995. The Maintenance Contribution Collection Agency will then seek to recover the money from the non-resident parent. Maintenance was previously collected by the municipalities but the recovery rate was poor. The new Agency is unpopular but widely regarded as effective; around 80% of advance payments are recovered.

Current issues

There has been a debate about the extent to which contact arrangements influence the payment of child support, but there is no hard data on this issue. A recent proposal to 'modernise' child support by, among other things, taking into account the income of both resident and non-resident parents and linking maintenance and contact more explicitly, was defeated. The new government is working on revised proposals.

Country profile: Sweden

Demography

Sweden has the lowest marriage rate of the countries in the review, and the highest age of women at first marriage. The divorce rate is in the middle range. Half of all births are to unmarried women, but it is known that many of these take place within cohabiting unions, and the rate of teenage births is amongst the lowest for the countries compared. Slightly under one in five families with children is headed by a lone parent.

Lone parent policy

Surveys and statistical analyses show that lone-parent families in Sweden are disadvantaged in many respects. Family policy has focused on protecting these economically vulnerable families, but since the 1980s there has been a general trend to ease the burden on non-resident parents and improve the situation for the second family, thus placing the responsibility for the first family on society at large.

Lone parents are not a strong lobby but their interests are powerfully supported by political and women's organisations. Non-resident parents on the other hand are a vociferous group and have benefited from changes made over the 1980s. As a result the Government has been keen to keep maintenance allowances for children down and encourage lone parents into work to supplement income payments.

Calculation of child support

Courts decide on the child maintenance award according to individual circumstances. There are also guidelines on how to calculate awards set by the Department of Social Welfare. If the parents agree the courts will simply ratify the parents' statement. Parents must contribute towards a child's needs in reasonable proportion to its needs and their combined capacity.

The child's needs are expressed as a proportion of a standard monthly amount, which is the basis for adult benefit rates, depending on age:

* *Aged 0-6 65% of standard monthly amount*
* *Aged 7-12 80%*
* *Aged 13+ 95%*

If the parents are in a position to provide more than the standard amount, then this is taken into account when assessing the child's needs. A parent is not liable to pay child support if he is not self-supporting so a deduction can be ordered for ordinary living expenses and reasonable housing costs. If there is a second family, the basic principle is to equate the needs of all the children, so that support to the first family is reduced.

Minimum amount

There is no minimum payment which is required of all non-resident parents.

Guaranteed payments

If payments are defaulted the lone parent can apply for maintenance support from the Department of Social Welfare, which the Department pays and then recoups from the non-resident parent. Unmarried mothers can also use this system without having a maintenance award from the courts. The maintenance advance is flat-rate, tax free and paid regardless of the employment and family circumstances of the resident parent. It is currently worth around £80 per month. Maintenance received is offset against the amount of maintenance support; lump sum payments of maintenance are apportioned and also reduce the amount payable. Maintenance support can be paid until children reach the age of 20 if they are still in full-time education.

Municipal social welfare departments are responsible for ensuring that paternity is established, and the mother must participate in this, to qualify for Maintenance Support. The service is efficient – paternity is established in 96% of cases – but receipt of benefit does not depend on whether paternity is actually established.

Recovery is sought from the non-resident parent according to the number of children, as a percentage of income:

- *10% for 1 child*
- *6.25% each for 2 children*
- *5% each for 3 children*

However, the amount recovered can never exceed the amount of maintenance support paid; this procedure does not generate a positive sum for the resident parent. Where the non-resident parent does not pay voluntarily the matter is referred to the crown bailiffs who collect monies by wage attachments, and also use income tax refunds.

Current issues

A question which has been raised is the equity of paying advance maintenance to resident parents who are well off. Means-testing was considered but rejected as having a negative effect on resident parents on low incomes, who make up the majority of lone parents, without offering significant public expenditure savings. The issue of whether it is reasonable to pay advance maintenance or child support when the resident parent is living with a new partner or remarries has also been discussed.

Because maintenance support supplements child support payments which are below this level, the current system has created a disincentive for the courts to set support awards appropriately unless the non-resident parent can provide more support than is provided through the advance maintenance benefit.

Recent changes allow social insurance offices to control certain types of avoidance by non-resident parents. For instance, income diverted into pensions and savings schemes continues to be counted as assessable income, and there is a general provision for maintenance to be assessed on a higher income than that reported if the non-resident parent does not appear to be exercising their earnings capacity (as in the case of directors drawing a small salary from a company for example).

Country profile: USA

Demography

The proportion of families with children headed by a lone parent is highest in the USA, at almost thirty per cent. The USA has the highest marriage rate and the highest divorce rate. Women marry on average two to three years younger than their counterparts in Europe, and somewhat over a quarter of all births are to unmarried women. The USA has by far the highest rate of births to teenage women: at 78 per thousand this is around twice as high as in the UK and the former GDR, the other countries with high numbers of teenage births, and almost ten times the rate for the Netherlands.

Lone parent policy

There are no specific benefits for lone parents in the USA. Parents who work can get a refundable tax credit (Earned Income Tax Credit) and families with insufficient resources may be eligible for time limited Temporary Assistance for Needy Families (TANF). To qualify the family must contain a child under 18, and be subject to deprivation due to the death, incapacity, unemployment or continued absence of a parent. Lone parents account for around 90 per cent of TANF claimants.

When a lone parent registers for TANF she or he must sign a declaration of intent to co-operate with the Child Support Enforcement Unit, provide relevant details, and sign a form giving rights to any maintenance received to the DTA. The parent can refuse if good cause can be demonstrated.

Although the funding for TANF is provided at the federal level, states have a considerable degree of discretion in establishing policy. In some states teenage mothers are required to live with their parents, and there is a large variation in the work requirements imposed on lone mothers.

Calculation of child support

Child support enforcement is run by the state and local human services departments who locate absent parents, establish paternity and obligations and enforce payment orders. Women's movements have been active in pressing for legislation on child support and in campaigning for greater enforcement.

1993 legislation laid down a requirement that states establish hospital-based programmes as a way of establishing paternity early in a child's life. These have been successful, although they have only managed to maintain, rather than increase, the proportion of fathers liable for child support, as the proportion of extra-marital births has also increased.

States use a variety of calculation methods; some use an administrative formula, but the majority use a percentage of income. Amounts assessed appear to be similar regardless of the system used.

Enforcement

Enforcement measures available include intercepting income tax refunds of non-paying parents, deductions from earnings, and revocation of driving licences. However, it is not clear how much they are used. Non-resident parents who have defaulted on maintenance payments are given three options: pay up, go to jail, or spend 16 weeks in an unpaid community work experience.

Some states have even displayed 'Wanted Lists' of parents who owe child support in post offices to reinforce the message that evasion of child support responsibilities is a serious offence.

Minimum amount

Some states require a minimum payment even where the non-resident parent is unemployed.

Guaranteed payments

There is no generally guaranteed payment. Only child support collected can be transferred to the resident parent. The Wisconsin guarantee system is an exceptional case.

Current issues

About 60 per cent of lone mothers had child support orders in both 1978 and 1991, and the average order amount, adjusted for inflation, was lower in 1991 than 1978. There been no improvement in the percentage of families receiving payments during this period. Case by case handling also resulted in a system that worked differently for poor fathers than for rich fathers: those able to afford a good lawyer paid less, and the minimum amount was also set in such a way that it accounted for a larger proportion of the earnings of the low paid.

Personal Responsibility and Work Opportunity Act 1996 (PRWOA) contains the provisions passed by Congress to strengthen state child support collection. Under this Act each state must operate a child support enforcement programme meeting federal requirements in order to be eligible for block grants for social assistance. The new provisions include a national new hire reporting system (where states send details of newly recruited staff for computer matching against lists of non-paying parents so that deductions can be made from wages). The legislation also streamlined paternity establishment, and created uniform interstate child support laws, computerised state-wide collections, new penalties (revoking drivers' and professional licences, seizing assets and community service, as well as garnishment [deduction from wages] orders), and grants to programmes improving access and visitation of non-resident parents.

States vary dramatically in the extent to which they are successful in recovering maintenance due; some states collect as few as 10 per cent of court orders. The federal government has spent $2 billion setting up new computer systems to help various states track non-paying fathers, but only 12 states have workable systems in place. Almost nine in ten states do not have the infrastructure to cope with collection. Politicians are increasingly calling for child support enforcement to be handled by the Internal Revenue System.

5

Lessons for child support policy

The next phase in the life of the Child Support Agency will be a crucial one. Having resisted repeated calls for the Agency's abolition, the Government has set itself the thankless task of making substantive changes to child support policy. Some commentators (see, for instance, Maclean 1998) have argued that the policy would in any case now begin to 'bed down'; the passage of time, together with the changes introduced in 1995, are seen as sufficient to gain broad acceptance from the public. The majority, however, still feel that significant reform is required. The range of people with an interest in the outcomes of policy reform is broad. As well as the specific interest groups such as NACSA and Families Need Fathers, this includes not only government departments, and those parents who are directly affected by the policy, but taxpayers as a whole, including families on modest incomes who are perceived as resenting the costs of providing for children whose parents do not meet their maintenance commitments. This chapter considers the lessons which can be learnt both from UK child support policy to date, and from the experiences of other countries, and the extent to which these are reflected in the changes proposed in the Green Paper, *Children First* (Department of Social Security, 1998b).

Child support and family policy

UK child support policy, like that of Australia and the USA, is focused on securing private arrangements for the payment of maintenance, an approach which Millar (1996) has characterised as typically 'Anglo-Saxon'. By contrast, European child support systems are embedded in a range of policies concerned with child rearing, which include not only cash transfers and tax allowances, but a range of services in kind. These family policies are often linked to official estimates of the cost of raising a child and reflect explicit expectations about the division of financial responsibility for children between the State and the family. Childcare provision, maternity and childcare leave provision, labour market demand, and the level of (female) wages are all relevant here. If women enjoy equality in the labour market, and a generous package of support for children, as in the Nordic countries, they have less need of private maintenance, although this may be at the expense of undervaluing their unpaid work in the home. Fagnani (1998) argues that maintenance has not become an issue in France because of high rates of maternal employment, and the package of benefits and childcare services which supports such employment.

In the UK, family policy is implicit, and financial responsibility for children has traditionally been seen as primarily a private, rather than a public, responsibility. Child support makes the cost of raising children visible and contentious, by exposing what is normally hidden within individual family finances: in so doing it creates the need to resolve issues about both the level of support for children which is reasonable, and where its costs should fall. In addition to balancing the claims of first and second families, the incomes of resident and non-resident parents and the costs of children to their individual families and to the tax-payer, decisions must also be made about the scope of the system, methods of calculation and enforcement, and a range of other factors.

The scope of child support policy

UK child support policy was conceptualised and designed as part of social security policy. This had a number of implications for the form of the policy instruments which emerged. It played a major role in the decision to use a complex administrative formula to determine the amount of maintenance, and for the formula to be linked to the amounts used for the calculation of benefit. The fact that the policy was steeped in a 'benefits culture' may also have contributed to the alienation of middle-class 'customers' of the Agency who were unused to a high level of intrusion into their personal and financial arrangements. These problems are linked to an overall perception of the social security system in the UK as residual, which gives a very different sense of 'ownership' from that which exists in countries such as Austria and Norway.

As in many other countries, use of the Child Support Agency is mandatory for those claiming means-tested benefits, but optional for those who are not. This also affects the former partners of those currently on benefit: the sheer number of people who were potentially affected by the legislation appears to have been under-estimated at the time of its introduction. Much of the debate centred on lone parents, and far less attention was paid to those couple families where there were children from previous relationships – together both groups account for almost 30 per cent of all families with dependent children. Moreover, those living in 'reconstituted' families, and not claiming benefit, were not accustomed to official intervention in their daily lives.

There is some evidence that couples who are able to do so are increasingly by-passing the Agency, and making their own arrangements (Deas, 1998). It is not clear to what extent the proposed percentage formula will allow couples to make private arrangements; there are a number of advantages to doing so. Not only would the reduction in the client load assist the running of the Agency and reduce costs, but some of those who would be removed from its scope are currently its most vocal and time-consuming critics.

As we have seen, several countries allow parents to opt out of using the child support scheme provided that the sum agreed does not fall below a certain minimum level, and agreements of this type are not subject to revision if a subsequent claim to benefit is made, thus avoiding the problems of retrospective effect which have been so damaging in the UK context. The level of payments is usually linked to amounts paid in guaranteed maintenance, or to the lowest figures generated by support tables, and therefore tend to be rather low, typically around £70.00 to £90.00 per month. In countries such as Norway and Australia, where the policy aim is for parents to reach private arrangements, most use the Agency. This may be connected with the amounts of support available, although it may also reflect issues of collection and enforcement. In the Netherlands, a fee of ten per cent is charged to the non-resident parent on mainte-nance collected through the Agency, as an incentive to make private arrangements.

Deciding how much non-resident parents should pay

UK child support legislation appears to have been based on fundamental misconceptions about the ability of non-resident fathers to pay maintenance for their children. The survey of maintenance recipients carried out in preparation for the White Paper had identified the large proportion of absent parents who were receiving benefits themselves. The difficulties of extracting 'quarts from pint pots' are widely acknowledged – in a situation where a family now requires one and a half wages in order to achieve a reasonable standard of living, trying to make one wage meet the needs of two families is doomed to failure. Thus child support can only ever represent part of an overall strategy for meeting the financial needs of children.

One of the problems in deciding how much it is reasonable for a parent to pay is an absence of consensus in the UK on the costs of bringing-up children and on who should bear those costs. A related issue, and one which is more rarely discussed, is when the obligation to pay maintenance for a child should stop. In a society where young adults are leaving home later, and require increasing amounts of financial support whilst in further and higher education, removing the maintenance obligation at an early age may have inequitable results for the custodial parent. Increasingly, other European countries are recognising a need for maintenance until the completion of tertiary education, although such payments are not usually compulsory.

The 1991 Child Support Act sought to increase average weekly payments from around £25.00 to around £45.00. The average weekly amount of maintenance paid has in fact stabilised at a figure not far above that paid prior to the introduction of the policy and which is broadly comparable to average amounts of maintenance paid in other European countries (Corden, forthcoming). Is one of the lessons which has been learnt that this is the level of maintenance which can be expected, and that attempts to obtain more are likely to be costly, controversial and largely ineffective? The fact that the average amount of maintenance which will be payable under the proposed reforms is estimated at £30.00 per week appears to support this conclusion.

The extent to which policy is perceived as fair plays a large part in securing its legitimacy with the public. This affects not only the level of individual compliance, but also, at a broader level, what has been described as the public's 'consent to be ruled' (Bradshaw, 1996). The existing maintenance formula was painstakingly designed to be consistent and to take account of a huge variety of circumstances. However, its complexity has meant that it is not transparent: people cannot understand how their maintenance has been assessed, which undermines their acceptance of it as fair. As had been widely canvassed beforehand, the Green Paper proposes to replace the formula with a simple percentage of net income, depending on the number of children: 15 per cent for one child, 20 per cent for two children and 25 per cent for three or more children. Those with earnings below £200.00 per week will pay a reduced amount. No allowance is to be made for housing costs or other regular outgoings, which are assumed to be met from the income remaining. This removes a significant loophole which some non-resident parents have been able to use to reduce their child support liability. It is not clear to what extent the system will be able to deal with the problems of under-reported income from self-employment.

Problems may be anticipated with a simple formula, as some people interpret fairness in terms of taking account of individual circumstances, such as the costs of contact, housing and education. All the changes made to the original formula to date have increased the range of circumstances which are taken into account. Some fathers' groups have already responded to proposals for simplification with cries of 'rough justice'. Experience from the US, however, suggests that these concerns may be misplaced, since what appear to be very different methods of assessment actually produce rather similar sums in practice (Garfinkel, 1998). Political pressures may be hard to resist, however, and other elements may need to be put in place in order to secure public acceptance of this change. For instance, in Australia and the US, a 'departures' system was set in place from the outset. The Green Paper proposes allowing tribunals to make orders which vary from the percentage formula in certain cases, such as where the non-resident parent makes contributions to housing costs, or where a child living with them is disabled and has additional costs. What is not clear at this stage is how prescriptive any guidelines will be, and whether it be possible to prevent such tribunals from becoming a means of diluting the general principle of the simplified formula.

It is also proposed to make all non-resident parents, including prisoners where they have earnings, pay a minimum amount of £5 per week in child support. There are large differences of opinion between those who feel that liable parents should be required to make a contribution to maintenance even where they are on very low incomes, and those, generally from the 'poverty lobby', who feel that requiring payments in such situations is not only inequitable but uneconomic. Changes in Australia in 1997 made such payments mandatory for all (Funder, 1997). Those who are in favour of universal payments point to their symbolic or moral value in honouring the child support obligation, and in creating a normative expectation of payment. The latter function may be important if the obligation first arises during a period of low income (Meyer, 1997) but it is impossible to predict any effects in advance. The payment of 'symbolic' amounts of maintenance may also be deemed important as a signal to taxpayers about the seriousness with which the policy is being pursued. However, as the costs of collection will generally outweigh the income, this could also be viewed as a rather expensive public relations exercise.

Fairness between families

In allocating financial responsibility for children between separated parents, it is possible to apportion this, either equally, or by reference to criteria such as the relative earnings or caring responsibilities of the resident and non-resident parent. The suggested reforms explicitly *exclude* any consideration of the income of the resident parent in assessing the amount of maintenance due. In opting for this course, the UK has taken the same path as Germany and Austria, where the day-to-day care provided by the resident parent is assumed to fulfill their share of the support obligation. Alternatives include taking account of both parents' income, as recently proposed (and ultimately not adopted) in Norway (which ignores the value of the resident parent's unpaid work in the home) and taking account of the income of the resident parent only above a certain threshold (as in Australia).

The Green Paper aims to take what it describes as a 'even-handed' approach to the issue of children in first and second families. Two potential approaches to the calculation of the maintenance obligation are discussed.

The first involves treating children in each family as if they were the sole qualifying family, so that, for instance, where there is one child in each family, each would be entitled to 15 per cent of the non-resident parent's income. Whilst this appears neutral, it favours second families, since the percentage would be applied in two steps, with the first family receiving a percentage of the amount which remained **after** the deduction for the second family. This inequality becomes more marked if there are more children in the second family than the first.

The second approach, which appears to be less favoured by the Government, would treat two children living in separate households as if they were in a single qualifying family, so that maintenance obligation would be assessed at 20 per cent of income, which would be divided equally between the children. Whilst this latter option may appear more equitable, it generates smaller sums of maintenance. For instance, under the first option, a man earning £300 a week would pay £38 to one child living elsewhere, and would keep £262, of which £45 would be the notional maintenance for one child living with him, whereas under the second, he would pay £30 and retain £270. The question of whether or not first families should have a priority claim on income in principle should be resolved.

There are two possible sources of inequity implicit in the overall approach to the issue of second families. Resident parents with high earnings will remain entitled to maintenance even where they are substantially better-off than non-resident parents. Whilst this is likely to affect only a minority of parents, it could make for some high-profile negative media coverage. Secondly, and more significantly, by reducing the average amount of maintenance payable, the reforms will favour a second family, with two potential earners, over a lone-parent family, whose sole potential earner is faced with continuing discrimination and low wages in the labour market.

Supporting parental relationships

The child support legislation intervenes in areas of people's lives which are painful and emotionally distressing, but the implications of this appear to have been under-estimated at the time the policy was introduced. One well-documented effect of UK child support legislation has been the souring of previously co-operative relationships between separated parents (Clarke *et al.*, 1996; Davis *et al.*, 1998). Child support policy needs to be framed in such a way as to allow families to move on from the painful process of separation and negotiate patterns of relating which avoid blame and bitterness. Indeed, given the links which exist between good relationships and the payment of maintenance, negative outcomes in relationships may be counter-productive even in a narrowly financial sense.

The debate about child support has tended to cast non-resident fathers in the role of scapegoat. There is evidence that a great many men do lose touch with their children following relationship breakdown, but the reasons are complex, and do not necessarily imply lack of interest; those who do remain in contact often do so at considerable financial and personal cost (Simpson *et al.*, 1995; Bradshaw *et al.*, 1999). Bradshaw *et al.* (1999) identified more willingness to pay maintenance amongst men who had contact with their children. Evidence from the United States, however, (Meyer, 1997) suggests that although there is a strong correlation between contact and maintenance, there is no evidence of a causal relationship, and both behaviours are likely to be the result of a third factor, such as the quality of the parent–child relationship, length of time since separation, geographical proximity and so on. One important influence on the commitment to payment of maintenance identified by Meyer (1997) is whether it was paid during the first year of liability.

Legal obligations may not match the ways in which people in changing family formations perceive their obligations to each other (Millar and Warman, 1996). This is borne out by the experience of the Child Support Act, which defined biological parenthood as absolutely unconditional, while the available evidence suggests that parents themselves see things rather differently. The fact that UK policy appears to have been designed primarily to cope with the needs of divorcing couples, at a time when the main growth in lone parenthood was amongst those who had never married, may have created particular problems in this respect. Countries where cohabitation and lone parenthood are widespread are increasingly tending to vest legal rights and duties in parental, rather than couple, status (Kiernan and Estaugh, 1993; Millar and Warman, 1996; Ditch *et al.*, 1997) and there is some evidence that such thinking has had an influence in the UK, as evidenced by the suggestion (Burgess, 1998) that parents enter binding contractual relationships with their children, and the recent decision, by the Lord Chancellor's Department, to extend parental responsibility to unmarried fathers who are registered on the child's birth certificate.

The issue of linking parental rights and parental duties, whether at an individual or societal level, is a complex one. The idea of maintenance being seen to 'buy' contact with children is one which rightly raises ethical and child welfare concerns, and has led to an emphasis on the need for a separation of the two issues. At the same time, strong pressures to link maintenance and contact have been created by groups campaigning against the Child Support Agency such as Families Need Fathers and NACSA. The Green Paper proposes lowering the threshold for the reduction of the maintenance obligation from the current 104 days per year overnight stay with the non-resident parent to 52 per year, a development which is likely to be welcomed by groups representing these parents.

Enforcement

The provision for resident parents to be exempted from the requirement to co-operate with the Agency in situations where this would cause 'harm or undue distress' to themselves or a child is one which has become viewed as a major weakness in the scheme, with as many as seven in ten benefit claimants initially refusing to co-operate (Department of Social Security, 1998). There have been suggestions that police evidence should be required to substantiate claims of violence. Recent evidence from Australia (Shaw, 1997) suggests that such a strategy would put women at increased risk, and any changes in the 'good cause' provisions should be subject to careful scrutiny. The creation of an incentive to co-operate, in the form of the new maintenance disregard for Income Support claimants, may prove to be sufficient to reduce the number alleging 'good cause'.

It is suggested that enforcement levels will be improved by requiring payment to the Agency by direct debit, standing order, or deduction from wages. The latter is to be pursued immediately payments are missed.

All countries with child support systems in place have problems dealing with the situation of the self-employed. As Boden and Corden (1998) have pointed out, the absence of a single measure for assessing self-employed earnings can result in both unrealistically high and unduly low assessments of ability to pay maintenance. Enforcement poses particular problems in the case of self-employed people, because it is not possible to use Attachment of Earnings orders. However, this is a nettle which must be grasped if the public are to perceive child support policy as fair; many complaints to the Independent Case Examiner from resident parents were concerned with this issue (Independent Case Examiner, 1998). A recent pilot scheme in one area has reported greatly increased compliance following intensive approaches to self-employed non-resident parents early in the process. This is shortly to be extended nationwide.

Creating winners

Child support policy needs to be able to balance the 'losers' from the policy against clearly defined 'winners'. One obvious reason for the widespread disillusionment with the Agency on the part of lone parents and their organisations is that the policy has failed to generate gains for women and children, since parents on Income Support receive no additional cash when maintenance is paid, whilst those already in work have not been treated as priority cases for the Agency. The proposed introduction of a £10.00 maintenance disregard for those on Income Support is therefore welcome. Targeting lone parents in employment also merits serious consideration, since evidence from abroad suggests that maintenance plays a stronger role in preventing lone mothers from returning to benefit than it does in helping them leave benefit initially (Meyer, et al., 1996). It is not clear from the Green Paper what timescale is now envisaged for extending the services of the Agency to those not currently on benefit.

If maintenance is intended to support the employment of lone parents, the reliability of payment may be as important as the amount. Resident parents argue that it is preferable to receive a small payment regularly than a large one infrequently (Hutton *et al.*, 1998). This has led to calls for a maintenance guarantee (Bennett, 1997), either for all parents with care, or for those on Family Credit. Offering a general maintenance guarantee is generally regarded as a costly option although some commentators (see Garfinkel, 1998) argue that this is not the case where most lone mothers are on Income Support, and it appears to have been ruled out in the medium term.

Instead, there will be provision to guarantee the incomes of families receiving Working Families Tax Credit, who would otherwise lose the incentive to work if maintenance was not paid. Precise details are yet to be announced. Whilst this guarantee is welcome as far as it goes, it implies the creation of a poverty trap for those whose earnings increase beyond the threshold for Working Families Tax Credit.

Marketing the policy

The existence of competing perspectives on the nature and extent of the child support obligation does not imply that attitudes and values cannot change, but it does mean that such a process, where it occurs, is likely to be gradual, and cannot simply be imposed overnight. In contrast to the 1990 White Paper, which merely asserted the responsibility of parents for their children, the recent Green Paper on the reform of child support recognises that child support issues can be contentious, and that a marketing exercise will be required. The language of the Green Paper itself is conciliatory: the emotive term 'absent parent' is replaced with the more neutral 'non-resident parent', and care is taken to stress the continuing involvement which many non-resident parents have with their children. The substance of the changes proposed aims to offer gains across the range of stakeholders, by reducing the amounts due from non-resident parents, ignoring the income of second partners, reducing maintenance bills to reflect contact costs, and allowing lone parents on benefits to keep a proportion of the maintenance paid. Overall, however, the effect of the reforms is to favour two-parent households at the expense of lone parents. As the latter group lack political and economic leverage, this may not prove a major obstacle to marketing the policy, but it is a weakness which may yet have consequences over the longer term.

Improving administration

Although this chapter has concentrated on the substance of child support policy, public acceptance of any policy is undermined by poor administration. The Child Support Agency has the unfortunate record of being the only government department ever to have been the subject of three separate enquiries by the Parliamentary Ombudsman's Committee. It has consistently accounted for a large volumn of MP correspondence and complaints to the Ombudsman. Factors leading to this situation included the departure of key individuals involved in policy development just as the policy was being implemented, the purchase of an inappropriate computer system, and the decision to recruit new staff, some of whom were totally inexperienced in administrative work. Recent research on the attitudes of Agency customers (Hutton *et al.*, 1998) suggests that although satisfaction levels are influenced primarily by the outcomes in individual cases, they could also be improved substantially by:

- improved communications, including more sensitively worded letters, and acknowledgement of correspondence;
- speedier assessments;
- small teams able to provide a personal service to customers.

The first annual report of the Independent Case Examiner (Independent Case Examiner, 1998) makes similar recommendations.

Conclusion

Child support raises issues of gender equity, as well as financial, emotional and moral responsibility for children, not all of which are likely to be resolved in the short term. Women are still the primary carers of children both within partnerships and following separation and divorce. Lone mothers face economic disadvantage in the labour market, and generally enjoy a much poorer standard of living than their former partners, even in the Scandinavian countries, where rates of employment are high. Yet there are signs that an increasing number of men and women do not wish child support arrangements to reinforce the situation of economic dependence which may have existed during a partnership. Over the longer term, enabling financial and emotional responsibility for children to become genuinely shared is likely to require an increased commitment to gender equality in both the private and public sphere, not only to redress the economic disadvantage faced by mothers, but in order to allow men the opportunity to be more involved and effective fathers.

Consultation with a wide range of stakeholders, an element which was lacking at the time the existing child support policy was introduced, will be an essential part of the reform process. There appears to be a genuine commitment to consultation on the proposed reforms, and a process of dialogue has begun. However, a considerable diversity of opinion about the best way forward remains, and no solution is likely to please all parties. Hard choices will have to be made, and more importantly, maintained, in the face of considerable pressure, if the Agency is to deliver benefits to either lone parents or the public purse.

6 Lessons for public policy-making

Introduction

Many central government policies advance through their development with the noises of tuning and adjustment scarcely audible outside Whitehall and the Houses of Parliament: thus they make their way through a range of consultation procedures and Select Committees into legislation and implementation. Rarely do these routine processes become sufficiently interesting to attract the attention of policy analysts. What is of most interest are those policies which create a public stir, are unpopular, and perform badly in operation. The child support policy is one such case. It raised public hostility during its making and fell into even greater disrepute immediately the administrative agency began operating. This chapter looks at the three main questions usually asked of problematic policies. First, can problems be foreseen, and therefore avoided? Second, can we feed other countries' positive experiences into our policy making? Third, can we learn enough from problematic policies to avoid making future mistakes? In what follows we look at each of these questions in turn.

Foreseeing and avoiding problems

We have seen in earlier sections of this report that the question of what went wrong and which factors were most to blame for the problems in child support policy were recalled by people involved in developing and implementing the policy. It was clear that, early on in the process, some negative signals were emerging and were either misjudged or under-estimated by the policy-makers. To this extent it can be said that part of the policy-making process was done unwisely. Policy development, for example, could have taken more account of negative reactions from the press and pressure groups to parts of the maintenance formula. Moreover, given the amount of effort put into the implementation of the policy, it would be not unreasonable to assume that more of the operational problems should have been anticipated. But although, as is clear from Chapter 3, some difficulties were anticipated, and mistakes were recognised at an early stage, on the whole the sheer intensity of the problems looming was not foreseen at the time. Discussions with policy-makers and other key players suggest that hindsight is easier and more common than insight in policy-making. Furthermore, even hindsight does not answer all the questions. Weighing the different issues was difficult both for the people interviewed and for the analysts involved in the review. After a careful reckoning, the prizes for the most significant problems of child support policy must go jointly to policy unpopularity and operational chaos: both were anticipated to a degree but not avoided, for reasons which are discussed in more detail later in this chapter.

Learning from other countries

While many analysts agree that being able to foresee and avoid policy problems is harder to achieve in practice than in theory, some policy-making methods are adopted on the assumption that these improve the chances of success. For example, the theory is that sharing experiences between countries has a high potential for contributing to policy success; applying such knowledge is, however, more complex in practice. In a recent paper on the enthusiasm for cross-cultural policy learning, Rudolf Klein offered a note of caution on the dangers of confusing learning *about* others experiences with learning *from* them.

> *'None of us can escape the bombardment of information about what is happening in other countries ... There is the systematic diffusion of information by OECD and other international organisations. There is the annual pilgrimage of academics from conference to conference. There are the formal contacts between politicians and civil servants within the framework of the European Union and other international organisations ... Learning about other countries must, of course, be sharply distinguished from learning from their experiences. The former activity is about collecting information; the latter is about reflecting on that information'* **(Klein, 1997).**

Klein's cautionary observations are borne out, to a large extent, by the findings of this review. Most of the key players interviewed recalled the enthusiasm in Whitehall for expeditions to find out what other countries were doing about child support. Learning about different cultural responses to what appear to be similar dilemmas rates highly for public servants – politicians and officers alike – and is seen as part of their job. But what appears to have been missed, or at least not fully taken into account at the time, was that child support systems in other countries had been set up on different premises and devised within different social structures: policies were grounded firmly in specific cultural contexts and there was little basis for comparison and transfer unless these factors were taken into account.

Furthermore, child support systems outside the UK were being recommended before these had been fully tested. Some of the good news about successful policies in other places was brought back to the UK before problems had emerged. As in the UK, some policies are better in theory than in practice and it is now clear that there are similar problems of operation and enforcement in child support systems cross-nationally: the observation of inappropriate comparisons is, like much about policy learning, better for a large dose of hindsight. What does hold true is that exposure to other countries' policy experiences is useful on two levels. First, it is broadly instructive and at a more general level of exchange adds value to home-grown policy-making. And second, it is likely that taking a look at common problems rather than policy development might well provide considerable scope for policy learning. The issue of problems inherent in the policy itself is explored in more detail later in the chapter.

Learning from our mistakes

We come now to the question of the future. If we can be sufficiently wise only after the event of a policy disaster, is there any way we can transfer this hard-won wisdom to the making of new policies? Can we learn from mistakes and get future policies right? There are two main issues here. The first is that weighing precisely the importance of specific parts of a policy in its success or failure is difficult. A second, but related issue is that policies do not consist of discrete entities. It is difficult, therefore, to know which parts of a policy contain unique failure factors: problems and mistakes compound each other (as do successes) in the policy process. These restrictions imply limits to learning from policy mistakes. Even with hindsight, as key players observed, individual child support problems flowed and merged into a larger chaos.

Some barriers will remain in policy-making even if factors of success and failure are properly identified. For example, we cannot eliminate all policy problems by increasing awareness of pitfalls and enhancing policy-making skills. Policy failure is not necessarily an indictment of design or manufacture: it may just as easily indicate the intrinsic difficulty of a policy idea and the sensitivity and complexity of the issues involved. Child support, for example, can involve two separate and often incompatible policy processes. On the one hand, maintenance assessment arising out of divorce, separation and relationship breakdowns calls for an individual, and often legal settlement. On the other hand, children and lone parents in receipt of social security benefits require a State administered maintenance system. Where maintenance cases straddle both systems, we face problems of complexity and confusion. But the problems do not disappear where cases fall neatly into either the system dealing with benefit recipients or that dealing only with non-benefit recipients. Here, problems change form and give rise to accusations of inequity, discrimination and 'two tier-ism': one system for the rich and another one for the poor. Even greater complexity occurs when cases which start out as non-benefit cases, and are thus deemed to be legal and private matters rather than administrative and public issues, subsequently become benefit cases. The intervention of public policy in what had been seen as a private and settled case has already been noted as a major cause of dissent.

Child support policy not only involves complex processes, but the issues surrounding it are highly charged. This may mean that no policy will ever please everyone and no one organisation will ever be able to administer it efficiently and effectively. Nor, as we have discussed, are all parents convinced of their duty to provide financial support to children with whom they do not live and with whom they may feel no legal or affective ties. This complex and emotional issue may not be amenable to changes of heart, at least not by means of public policy.

A final thought on learning for the future is to consider the limits of using policies as investments in a wider cultural change. This type of policy-making is not unusual and has been employed by a variety of governments in bids to influence the life and work habits of sections of the population. But these policies have a natural tendency to become unpopular early in their development and to need careful handling. The poll tax, for example, was one such policy, designed to include greater numbers of the population in financial responsibility for local public services. The cultural change was rejected and the policy was resisted and quickly extinguished by its unpopularity. Similarly, one of the drivers in child support policy ie. making parents financially responsible for their children, implied a far wider social change in the behaviour of, mainly young, men and women towards family relationships and work. Both Conservative and Labour governments share these expectations for cultural and social change and face similar barriers to successful policy-making towards this end. There are also warning lights for the making of the more recent welfare-to-work policies and their wider social implications. Early pressure group activity and the creating of unpopularity has already begun, and is unlikely to go away since the policy heavily implies a cultural shift in attitudes to work and employment for large numbers of people.

For all such policies, unless the unpopularity factor is anticipated and taken account of, failure is likely for both long-term and immediate policy aims. As we noted earlier, however, overcoming unpopularity is more difficult than creating popularity from the outset. As with the poll tax, when the effects of unpopularity become debilitating, the overall cost of getting the policy to work may be too great. The costs of policy-making should include, therefore, a calculation of the political and financial investment and an estimate of their limits. In cases where the costs are calculated as too high, a policy may have to be taken back to the drawing board or dropped altogether.

General observations about policy-making

The final part of this chapter looks at broader policy-making ideas and practices and discusses whether policy problems can be anticipated, and to what extent it is possible to learn lessons from abroad or from past mistakes. It draws on observations about changes in policy-making over the past ten years or so, and provides a brief account of some of the policy thinking of the 1990s together with some analytical observations. This section contains some well-known and well-aired truisms which are, nevertheless, essential to this discussion: it is sometimes necessary to restate obvious truths to remind us not to ignore them when analysing policy.

Policy-making within and between departments

The first observation is that individual policies are not made in isolation from other policies within government departments. This has major implications, both for policy analysis and for future learning. As we discussed earlier, it is very difficult to pinpoint specific reasons behind the impetus for a policy: policies unfold, whether slowly or at speed, out of all sorts of ideas. Furthermore, developing, adjusting and fine-tuning policies is likely to have effects on other policy areas. As has been shown earlier in interviews with people who played key roles in the development of the child support policy, the issues surrounding the Child Support Act and the creation of an administrative agency at the beginning of the 1990s were varied and complex, and about more than just the financial care of children. But governments are prompted to take an interest in demographic and population trends as much by chance encounter with departmental and academic statistics as by design or purpose. As we have noted already, child support policy began its development alongside the concern of policy makers about an increasingly complex and incoherent benefits system, and the rising cost of benefit payments.

The second observation from the study was that the manufacture of some policies does not fall exclusively to one government department: policy-makers in the lead department consult and work with other departments. Many aspects of policy-making increasingly need to be shared. Although this would seem a sensible way of going about policy-making, Whitehall is sometimes surprisingly reluctant to go beyond the simple mechanics of departmental co-operation. It is a simple matter to arrange inter-departmental meetings between officers where pledges to co-operate are exchanged. It is entirely another thing to exchange organisational confidences and provide insights into internal policy failures. The making of the child support policy provided an interesting illustration of this limited exchange where policies straddle several departments. We noted in an earlier chapter that policy-makers in the Department of Social Security experienced a reluctance on the part of the Treasury to bend their rules on the rate of return expected on investment in the new external agencies. There was no way that the Treasury could find to ease the path of the Child Support Agency even though it fell quickly into quite severe operating difficulties. But this particular inter-departmental tension was said to be standard Treasury practice and not aimed specifically at child support policy.

But there were also tensions between the DSS and other departments. The search for a new child support system was, as we have already discussed, part of a wider concern with a chaotic benefits system, as well as unacceptable maintenance settlements made by an expensive and equally chaotic legal system. This gave the policy an inter-departmental context, although there were differences of opinion over which department could provide the best stewardship of the policy. Eventually, the policy was housed within the DSS for administrative purposes, but consultation with the Lord Chancellor's Department continued. Some key players recalled that once the decision was made to locate the policy in the DSS, the co-operation between departments appeared less than whole-hearted. Experiences of the more negative aspects of operating maintenance systems, for instance, were not shared. Albeit with the benefit of hindsight, some key players thought that a more open relationship between departments would have enabled policy-makers to understand more about the job they were taking on: an advance knowledge of the complexities of assessment and the problems of enforcement might possibly have avoided some of the administrative pitfalls.

Similarly, key players recalled that a more detailed discussion about the reluctance of the Inland Revenue to take on any of the child support policy would have given the DSS more clues as to the difficult task they were undertaking. Some crucial facts about tax assessment and collection would have informed DSS policy-making, particularly the setting up and operation of the Agency. First, there were long-standing problems in assessment of tax owed by some people and even greater difficulties in gaining payment. Second, the Revenue recognised child support as an emotionally charged issue and a policy minefield. Their 'politically incorrect' line was that benefit clients were a problematic subset of the population at large and as such would be even less likely to pay what they owed. Although the Revenue's attitude to involvement in child support payments was known by some key players, a more open discussion of their reluctance to take part might have told policy-makers much about the operational problems ahead: child support policy was made without the benefit of a detailed and open examination and discussion of the limited success of tax debt collection in the UK. In an recent article about Whitehall culture in general, David Walker, the policy analyst and journalist, referred to the enduring separateness of departments in Whitehall as 'a system that is remarkably plural and veers towards the anarchic' (Walker, 1998). His conclusion was that 'departmentalism does rule, OK.'

Walker gave the example of one group of civil servants not minding embarassing another group, and suggested that 'somebody in a high place needs urgently to set out the rationale for government's internal diversity'. It is important to note here that the Labour Government, after one year's operational experience, shares Walker's view that policy-making is less than co-ordinated within Whitehall. The latest ministerial re-organisation (July 1998) has created a new Ministerial Co-ordinator (renamed 'the enforcer' by the media) to smooth the policy-making path in both Whitehall and the Cabinet Office. The job of this Minister will be to note well the inter-departmental holes in policy-making, at all stages, and make sure that they are mended.

Popularity and the culture of fairness

Observation number three is that policies can be difficult or impossible to implement because they are unpopular, and that some factors causing unpopularity can be distin-guished from those associated with inappropriate operational structures. This differentiation is a vital aid to problem-solving in policy-making. If a policy is regarded as essential but unpopular, ways may have to be found to make the policy acceptable to people. Unpopularity can be generated, for example, by the disapproval of pressure groups which perceive the policy to be to their disadvantage. In this case serious thought must be given as to how best a policy line can be held against such lobbies in order that a wider public debate can be carried out. Most lobbies, with the powerful backing of press and media, can skew public opinion against a policy and bring about its downfall before it has been properly aired, evaluated and modified. As discussed in an earlier chapter, policies with implications for dramatic social change may become subject to intense lobby pressure and media antagonism. Policies for welfare to work and child support, for instance are of this kind. They are both highly charged and controversial and are thus liable to fall into rapid unpopularity.

Another kind of unpopularity can be kindled by the pursuit of party politics and, just as with the lobbies, policy-makers may have to try to hold a policy line against political distortion. Politicians in opposition may agree with a government policy but at the same time work for it to be defeated. In other words, there is a temptation for politicians of all parties to sacrifice a good policy in the interests of party politics.

Observation number four is that the concept of fairness dominates much thinking in policy-making. In particular, in social security and also in social services, the concept of social justice is deeply embedded in policy-making traditions. To a lesser but growing extent, the notion of rights, entitlements and fairness is entering the health policy field. The recently aired notion of rationing and resource allocation in health services has become part of the policy analysts' study: so too are the longstanding but little discussed variations in health services between geographical areas and the implications for equity. However, as discussed earlier, the interpretations of fairness are many and varied and their pursuit by different interest groups does not make for easy policy development. The latest Green Paper on child support attempts to simplify the formula for assessment while at the same time keeping it fair (Department of Social Security, 1998). However, the culture of rough justice does not sit easily with our social security tradition and it may not be easy to change. The pursuit of a simpler formula for the assessment of child support may continue to be seen as unfair by some groups. In this case, the changes in policy will have to be backed up with a positive and convincing sales pitch and a firm political resolve.

Operationalising policies

Observation number five is that smoothing the operational path and ensuring successful implementation is a vital part of policy-making. Much is already going on in Whitehall towards this end. Since the early 1990s, for example, there have been great advances in policy-making, with built-in structures for measuring and monitoring performance. Ironically, however, the techniques for outcome evaluation are more advanced than the development of systems to ensure these outcomes. What is needed is an operational structure designed not only to measure performance but to ensure a good one: good outcome indicators go a long way to good outcomes but by themselves are not a sufficient guarantee of good practice. The Child Support Agency provides a case in point. Set up with targets and performance measures, it nevertheless started out with many organisational difficulties, including inappropriate computer facilities and untrained staff. The latest progress report on the work of the Agency (Child Support Agency, 1998) gives a gloomy prognosis for the administrative and financial situation of the Agency. The report states that although the work of the Agency is improving, it still has a backlog of cases, some unacceptable delays on assessments – up to 18 months – and it still produces far too many errors. After five or so years of operation this suggests that any policy changes resulting in additional work would not be helpful at the present time.

The Child Support Agency, however, is not alone in its inability to meet performance standards. A range of public service organisations have unsatisfactory practice records, yet because they do not experience high levels of public scrutiny and disapproval, do not fall foul of Select Committee and Ombudsman reports to the same extent as the Child Support Agency. As we have already noted, tax collection has a less than perfect record but does not yet come under such close scrutiny by performance monitors as do the Next Steps Agencies. The courts also have a poor record of maintenance enforcement which remained invisible to public scrutiny until the 1980s when their performance was made the subject of an increasingly wider discussion. The difference between the two older systems and the newer child support administration is that the former both pre-date the fashion for performance measurement and have, therefore, lower operational profiles. The Child Support Agency, by contrast, is a product of the 1990s public accountability culture as well as a part of the experiment in 'arm's length' service delivery: it is highly visible, its activities are the object of close Parliamentary scrutiny and it is being asked to explain its inability to meet agreed performance targets. It is likely that this fashion for policy accountability is here to stay and that all policy-making will, from now on, include detailed and structured plans for monitoring activities and outcomes with built-in sanctions for bad performance.

Even with the benefit of up-to-date monitoring techniques and effective public scrutiny, the combination of unpopularity and complexity has given the Child Support Agency what one key player described as 'an impossible job'. Unlike the Inland Revenue, the Child Support Agency had to include detailed life-style judgements in individual maintenance calculations, including such issues as what is 'reasonable' expenditure on entertainment and food as well as housing and travel. Although the intention of the new Green Paper is a greatly simplified formula – the assessment will now be based on a straight percentage of the absent parent's income – there remains an element of negotiation, particularly for self-employed parents. The social security system as a whole was never intended to cope with such complex assessments. Rather, its traditional role is to make formulaic assessments based on income and entitlements, leaving aside judgements of lifestyle expenditure. A more simple assessment formula will be an attractive option, and one which is endorsed by the Agency itself.

The negative consequences of early policy consensus

One of the most surprising findings of the study was about the nature of policy principles and the effect of political consensus on policy development. There were several interesting but unexpected observations about the early public responses to child support and the consequences of a face-value acceptance of policy rhetoric. Speaking about the political debate (or lack of it) in the House of Commons, one key player noted that universal agreement on a policy principle does not necessarily make for a successful policy – and indeed, may have the reverse effect. This notion of the dangers of an early consensus was brought up by several people closely involved in the policy-making process. What these comments suggest is that some policies which have the potential for complexity and controversy fail, paradoxically, to get a proper debate precisely because they start out as uncontestable principles and ideas. In the initial presentation to Parliament, these policies are highly abstract and often cloaked in moral imperatives. For fear of looking foolish or immoral in public, no one, not least politicians, will argue against them. Neither is this early stage of development thought to be suitable for discussing the feasibility of a policy.

There are two main points to make about policies of this kind. First, the misleading appearance of simplicity and transparency is unintentional and not usually a device to achieve acquiescence: it is purely the way some policies take shape from ideas. Second, the implications of these embryo policies take a while to become widely apparent and, therefore, provoke slower reactions. It is only later when these policies are fleshed out that close scrutiny takes place and a proper debate highlights the areas of contention. It follows therefore that policies which begin with a high level of political consensus combined with little debate should give out danger signals to policy-makers of all kinds. The early consensus on the child support policy might well serve as a warning. Policy-makers were convinced early on that All-Party support for the idea indicated an unproblematic policy. What had escaped notice was that the policy was not being subjected to a detailed and thorough examination and, as a consequence, was developing without appropriate adjustments and modifications.

Great expectations: a changing sense of policy ownership

The final observation from our study is that the manufacture of public policies has changed radically in the UK in the 1990s. First, policy actors now include more than the politicians and civil servants who were the traditional policy actors, and has extended beyond the lobby groups who have long been an established part of the policy-making elite. There are new systems in place in both local and central government to aid and enhance public accountability, to augment the flow of information about policy-making at all stages of its development and implementation, and to inform the public of the implications of a policy and its operational performance. In this way, the ownership of policy-making has been extended through democratic processes grafted on to the Parliamentary system. These mechanisms for both public and Parliamentary scrutiny and accountability were created in the 1980s as part of a revitalised public management which included the establishment of House of Commons Select Committees and the Parliamentary Ombudsman. In the case of child support policy there is also the Independent Case Examiner, established in 1997 to deal with individual complaints about the operations of the Agency. In particular, the Social Security Select Committee of 12 March 1991 was, in the event, much more searching examination of the policy than were MPs in the House at the time: it was the Committee process rather than the traditional Parliamentary process which examined the policy on behalf of the public. Furthermore, it is the Select Committee on Public Administration and the Parliamentary Commissioner for Administration which have most closely monitored the work of the Child Support Agency and its performance in service delivery.

All these systems were designed to increase the transparency and visibility of policies as an extension of the work of MPs in the two Houses. Through this means, the wider public has been made increasingly aware of and, to a large extent, more involved in, areas of policy-making process once exclusive to political parties and civil servants. Moreover, Parliamentary debates are now televised (as are some Select Committee sittings) so that we can see, as well as read about in the press, who said what about a policy's aims and intentions and what explanations there are for success or failure.

It is clear from this study of UK child support policy that the last two decades have seen some major changes in our capacity to make policies that are workable: there are more of us involved in the process, there is greater access to information about policies, and there are new mechanisms and structures for monitoring the operation of policies.

The powerful pressure of increased expectations should not be under-estimated either. We have come to assume that we should be able to see what is happening and influence events, at least those which affect us directly. Despite this progress, there still remain limits to anticipating and avoiding policy problems. Unpopularity is a powerful negative influence in policy-making and cannot always be avoided, although there is a growing awareness of how it impedes policy-making. Governments are now taking seriously the idea of selling policies more widely than to the lobbies and pressure groups who were traditionally the main audience for the sales pitch. But in the case of wide and intransigent opposition to all or parts of a policy, it remains for governments to decide whether to press on or withdraw. Policy-making, although vastly improved in the last twenty years, has yet to find a way of designing out all the error factors either in advance or in a timely fashion during the process. Attributing reasons for the success or failure of a policy is still easier at a distance – with hindsight. Policy-makers are doing better but they are still looking for hints and clues on how to learn lessons and avoid future mistakes.

Future prospects for child support

We have seen that many of the problems encountered by the child support policy are not unique, but are shaped by traditions of policy-making and the conflicts of interest which are played out in the political process. Yet child support also poses specific dilemmas; it stands at the juncture of the public and private domains, and must operate across the spheres of welfare policy and family law in a highly charged and emotional area. The recent proposals for reform of child support represent a considered and well-argued response to the problems of balancing the interests of individual family members, and of responding to lobby pressures. Yet it is already becoming clear that they are generating a good deal of controversy and that they will be vulnerable to precisely the same kind of pressure which this chapter has identified. Success in design and implementation is by no means assured; and once again, can only be fully evaluated after the event.

Bibliography

Australian Department of Social Security (1997). *Child support scheme – what's new, what's different?* Melbourne: Department of Social Security

Bennett, F. (1997). *Child support. Issues for the future.* London: Child Poverty Action Group

Boden, R. and Corden, A. (1998, forthcoming). *Child support: measuring self-employed earnings.* London: HMSO

Bolderson, H. and Mabbett, D., with Hudson, J., Rowe, M. and Spicker, P. (1997). *Delivering Social Security: a cross-national study.* Department of Social Security Research Report No. 59. London: HMSO

Bowen, J. (1992). *Child support: the essential guide.* Queensland: Jacaranda Publishing

Bradshaw, J. (1996). Presentation to the All-Party Committee on the Child Support Act. University of York, Social Policy Research Unit

Bradshaw, J. and Millar, J. (1991). *Lone-parent families in the UK.* Department of Social Security, Research Report 6. London: HMSO

Bradshaw, J. and Stimson, C. (1996) *Fathers apart in Britain: preliminary results of a national survey.* Paper to the Australian Institute of Family Studies Conference, Brisbane, 27 November 1996

Bradshaw, J., Kennedy, S., Kilkey, M., Hutton, S., Corden, A., Eardley, T., Holmes, H., and Neale, J. (1996). *The employment of lone parents: a comparison of policy in 20 countries.* London: Family Policy Studies Centre

Bradshaw, J., Stimson, C., Skinner, C. and Williams, J. (1999, forthcoming). *Non-resident fathers in Britain.* London: Routledge

Brindle, D. (1997). Labour eyes child agency, *Guardian,* 25 April

Brown, C. and Abrams, (1998). Field hints at tax plan to replace Child Support Agency. *Independent,* 10 February 1998

Burgess, A. (1998). *A complete parent: towards a new vision for child support.* London: Institute for Public Policy Research

Burghes, L. (1991). *Supporting our children. The family impact of child maintenance.* Briefing Paper. London: Family Policy Studies Centre

Burghes, L. (1993a). *One-parent families. Policy options for the 1990s.* London: Family Policy Studies Centre

Burghes, L. (1993b). Lone parents – looking forward, looking back. *Family Policy Bulletin,* June. Family Policy Studies Centre

Burghes, L. (1993c). Child Support; *Family Policy Bulletin,* December. Family Policy Studies Centre

Burghes, L. (1995). Caught in the Act; *Family Policy Bulletin,* April. Family Policy Studies Centre

Burghes, L. and Brown, M. (1995). *Single lone mothers: problems, prospects and policies.* London: Family Policy Studies Centre

Castles, F. (ed) (1993). *Families of nations: patterns of public policy in western democracies.* Aldershot: Dartmouth

Chief Child Support Officer (1994, 1995, 1996, 1997). *Annual Report.* London: HMSO

Child Poverty Action Group (1993, 1994, 1995, 1996, 1997, 1998). *Child Support Handbook.* London: CPAG

Child Support Agency (1995, 1996, 1997, 1998). *Annual Report.* London: HMSO

Child Support Bill (1991). HL Bill 29. HMSO

Clarke, K., Craig, G. and Glendinning, C. with Thomson, M. (1993). *Children Come First? The Child Support Act and Lone Parent Families.* Child Care Consortium

Clarke, K., Glendinning, C. and Craig, C. (1994). *Losing support. Children and the Child Support Act.* London: Barnardo's and others

Clarke, K., Craig, C. and Glendinning, C. (1996). *Small change: the impact of the Child Support Act on lone mothers and children.* London: Family Policy Studies Centre

Clarke, L. (1996). Demographic change and the family situation of children. In Brannen, J. and O'Brien, M. (eds). *Children in families: research and policy, pp 66-83.* London: Falmer Press

Committee of Public Accounts (1988). The twenty-first report of the Child Support Agency. London: Stationery Office

Corden, A. (forthcoming). *Child maintenance schemes in Europe.* York: Social Policy Research Unit

Council on Tribunals (1995). *Annual Report 1993-94.* London: HMSO

Davis, G. Wikely, N., and Young, R. with Barron, J. and Bedward, J. (1998). *Child Support in Action.* Oxford: Hart

Deakin, N. and Parry, R. (1996/97). Images of the Tresury: the Treasury and social policy. Papers for the Whitehall Programme, 1996 and 1997. ESRC

Deas, Susan M. (1998). Family Lawyers Sidestep the CSA. *Family Law,* 48, January

Department of Social Security (1989). *Supplementary Benefit/Income Support Annual Statistical Inquiry.* London: HMSO

Department of Social Security (1990). *Children come first. The Government's proposals on the maintenance of children.* Government White Paper, Cm 1263. HMSO

Department of Social Security (1995a). Press release, 28 November. London: DSS

Department of Social Security, (1995b). *Improving child support.* Cm 2745. HMS.

Department of Social Security (1995c). *Child Support Agency quarterly summary of statistics,* November. London: DSS, Analytical Services Division

Department of Social Security (1996a). Press release, 2 April. London: DSS

Department of Social Security (1996b). Press release, 7 October. London: DSS

Department of Social Security (1996c). *Child Support Agency quarterly summary of statistics,* May. London: DSS, Analytical Services Division

Department of Social Security (1997). *Child Support Agency quarterly summary of statistics,* November. London: DSS, Analytical Services Division

Department of Social Security (1998a). *Child Support Agency quarterly summary of statistics,* February. London: DSS, Analytical Services Division

Department of Social Security (1998b). *Children first: a new approach to child support.* Cm 3992. London: HMSO

Ditch, J., Barnes, H. and Bradshaw, J. (1997). *A Synthesis of National Family Policies 1996.* York: Commission of the European Communities

Dopffel, P. (1988). Child support in Europe: a comparative overview. In Kamerman, S. and Kahn, A. (eds). *Child support – from debt collection to social policy.* London: Sage

Duncan, S. and Edwards, R. (1997). *Single mothers in an international context: mothers or workers?* London: University College Press

Eglin, D. (1998). Le recouvrement des pensions alimentaires. *Lettre CAF*, 81/98

Ergas, Y. (1990). Child care policies in comparative perspective: an introductory discussion. In Lone parent families: the economic challenge. *Social Policy Studies*, No.8. Paris: OECD

Esping-Anderson, G. (1990). *The three worlds of welfare capitalism.* Cambridge: Polity

Fagnani, J. (1998). 'Child support in France' paper presented at Family Policy Studies Centre seminar on 'The Development and Future of Child Support Policy', 26 February 1998.

Family Policy Studies Centre, (1996). *The Family Law Bill.* Family Briefing Paper 1. London: Family Policy Studies Centre

Ford, R. Marsh, A. and McKay, S. (1995). *Changes in lone parenthood.* Department of Social Security, Research Report No 40. London: HMSO

 Ford, R. and Millar, J. (eds) (1998). *Private lives and public responses: lone parenthood and future policy in the UK.* London: Policy Studies Institute

Fox Harding, L.M. (1996). Parental responsibility: the reassertion of private patriarchy? In Bortolaia Silva, E. (ed). *Good enough mothering? Feminist perspectives on lone motherhood.* London: Routledge

Funder, K. (1997). Changes in Child Support. *Family Matters No 48.* Melbourne: Australian Institute of Family Studies

Garfinkel, I. *et al.* (1997). The effects of child support on non-resident fathers: overview and summary. Paper presented at conference on 'The effects of child support enforcement on resident fathers', Princeton University, 13-15 September 1995 (and subsequently revised)

Garfinkel, I. *et al.* (1996). Deadbeat Dads or inept states? A comparison of child support enforcement systems. Unpublished paper.

Garfinkel, I. (1998). Lessons from the USA. Paper presented at Family Policy Studies Centre seminar on 'The Development and Future of Child Support Policy', 26 February 1998.

Garfinkel, I. and Wong, P. (1990). *Child support and public policy in lone-parent families. The economic challenge.* Paris: Organisation for Economic Co-operation and Development

Garnham, A. and Knights, E. (1994). *Putting the Treasury first: the truth about child support.* London: Child Poverty Action Group

Government response to the First Report from the Committee on Social Security on the operation of the Child Support Act (1994). Cm 2469. HMSO

Government response to the Social Security Committee Report on Child Support (1995). Cmnd 2743. HMSO

Government response to the Third Report of the Select Committee on the Parliamentary Commissioner for Administration (1995). 1994/95, Cm 2865. HMSO

The Guardian (1995). 'Sins against the fathers – CSA comes under fire for invading parents' privacy' 22 July 1995

Harrison, M. (1994). 'Child Support Reforms: the Australian Experience' *Family and Conciliation Costs Review* Volumn 32, number 2

Harrison, M., Snider, G. and Merlo, R. (1990). *Who pays for the children?* Australian Institute of Family Studies Monograph No 9

Haskey, J. (1998). One-parent families and their dependent children in Great Britain. *Population Trends*, 91

Her Majesty's Treasury (1989). *The Government's expenditure plans 1989-90 to 1991-92, Chapter 15, Department of Social Security.* London: HMSO

House of Commons Select Committee on the Parliamentary Commissioner for Administration (1995). First Special Report – Session 1995/96, HC 88. HMSO

House of Commons Select Committee on the Parliamentary Commissioner for Administration (1995). *The Child Support Agency,* Third Report, Session 1995/6 HC 199. HMSO

House of Commons Social Security Committee (1991). *Changes in maintenance arrangements: the White Paper 'Children Come First' and the Child Support Bill,* HC 277. HMSO

House of Commons Social Security Committee (1993). *The operation of the Child Support Act,* First Report – Session 1993/94, HC 690. HMSO

House of Commons Social Security Committee (1994). *The operation of the Child Support Act.* Second Report. HMSO

House of Commons Social Security Committee (1994). *The operation of the Child Support Act: proposals for change.* Fifth Report – Session 1993/94, HC 470. HMSO

House of Commons Social Security Committee (1994). First Report from the Social Security Committee, Session 1993-94, *The operation of the Child Support Act,* HC 69. HMSO

House of Commons Social Security Committee (1996). *The performance and operation of the Child Support Agency,* Second Report, Session 1995/96, HC 50. HMSO

House of Commons Social Security Committee (1996). *Child support: good cause and the benefit penalty.* Fourth report, Session 1995-96, HC 440. HMSO

House of Commons Social Security Committee (1996). *The performance and operation of the Child Support Agency,* Second Report – Session 1995/96, HC 470. HMSO

House of Commons Social Security Committee (1997). *Child support.* Fifth Report, Session 1996/7. HC 282. HMSO

Hutton, S., Carlisle, J. and Corden, A. (1998). *Customer views on service delivery in the Child Support Agency.* Department of Social Security Research Report No. 74. London: Stationery Office

Improving child support (1995). Government White Paper, Cm 2745. London: HMSO

Independent Case Examiner (1998). *Annual Report 1997/8.* Chester: Office of the Independent Case Examiner

Joint Select Committee on Certain Family Law Issues (1994). *Child support scheme – an examination of the operation and effectiveness of the scheme*

Kiernan, K. and Estaugh, V. (1993). *Cohabitation: extra-marital childbearing and social policy.* London: Family Policy Studies Centre

Klein, R. (1997). Learning from others: shall the last be first? *Journal of Health Politics, Policy and Law.* 22, 5, pp 1267-1278

Koren, C. (1998). Child support in Norway. Paper presented at Family Policy Studies Centre seminar on 'The Development and Future of Child Support Policy', 26 February 1998

The Law Society (1993). The Child Support Act: has it a future? Evidence to the House of Commons Social Security Committee. The Law Society's Family Law Committee

Lefaucheur, N. (1997). Qui doit nourrir l'enfant de parents non-mariés ou demariés. In *Recherches et Prévisions*, no 47. Paris: CNAF

Leira, A. (1996). *Parents, children and the state: family obligations in Norway.* Oslo: Institute for Social Research

Lewis, J. (ed) (1997). *Lone mothers in European welfare regimes: shifting policy logics.* London: Jessica Kingsley

Maclean, M. (1996). Financial obligations of parenthood: rules and choices. Unpublished paper. Centre for Socio-Legal Studies, Oxford

Maclean, M. (1998). In Ford, R. and Millar, J. (eds.) *Private lives and public responses: lone parenthood and future policy in the UK.* London: Policy Studies Institute

Maclean,M. and Eekelaar, J. (1997). *The parental obligation: a study of parental obligation across households.* Oxford: Hart

Marsh, A., Ford, R. and Finlayson, L. (1997). *Lone parents, work and benefits.* Department of Social Security Research Report no. 61. London: Stationery Office

Martin, C. (1997). L'action publique en direction des menages monoparentaux. In *Recherches et Prévisions*, No. 47. Paris: CNAF

McHugh, M. and Millar, J. (1997). Australia: supporting mothers to seek work. In Duncan, S. and Edwards, R. (eds), *Single mothers in an international context.*

McKay, S. and Marsh, A. (1994). *Lone parents and work.* Department of Social Security Research Report No.25. London: HMSO

Meyer, D. (1997). Compliance with Child Support Orders in paternity and divorce cases. Paper presented at symposium, 'The post-divorce family: research and policy issues', Lincoln, 30-31 May

Meyer, D and Hu, M-C. (1997). A note on the anti-poverty effectiveness of child support among mother-only families. Paper presented at the Public Affairs Workshop at the University of Wisconsin

Meyer, D. *et al.,* (1996). Child support reform: lessons from Wisconsin. *Family Relations,* January

Middleton, S., Ashworth, K. and Braithwaite, I. (1997). *Small fortunes – spending on children, childhood poverty and parental sacrifice.* York: Joseph Rowntree Foundation

Millar, J. (1996). Mothers, workers and wives: comparing policy approaches to supporting lone mothers in *Good enough mothering? Feminist perpectives on lone motherhood,* edited by Bortolaia Silva. London: Routledge

Millar, J. and Warman, A. (1995). *Defining family obligations in Europe* – national reports. Unpublished paper. University of Bath

Millar, J. and Warman, A. (1996). *Family obligations in Europe.* London: Family Policy Studies Centre

Ministry of Health and Social Affairs (1997). *Maintenance Support Act.* Stockholm: Ministry of Health and Social Affairs

NACAB (1994). *Child support: one year on*. CAN evidence. National Association of Citizens Advice Bureaux.

National Audit Office (1990). *Support for lone parents*. London: HMSO

National Audit Office (1995). Child Support Agency. Memorandum by the Comptroller and Auditor-General to the House of Commons Public Accounts Committee. London: HMSO

OECD (1995). *Main economic indicators*. Paris: OECD

Oldfield, N. and Yu, A. (1993). *The cost of children: living standards for the 1990s*. London: Child Poverty Action Group

Office of Population Censuses and Surveys (1993). *General Household Survey*, 1991. London: HMSO

Parliamentary Commissioner for Administration (1995). *Investigation of complaints against the Child Support Agency*, Session 1994/5, HC 135. London: HMSO

Parliamentary Commissioner for Administration (1996). *Investigation of complaints against the Child Support Agency*, Session 1995/6, HC 20. London: HMSO

Perkins, A. (1998). Divorce: pay to see children, *Guardian*, 10 February

Provan, B. *et al.* (1996). *The Requirement to Co-operate: a report on the operation of the 'good cause' provisions*. London: Child Support Agency

Reports of Standing Committee A (on Child Support Bill 1991), 11 June 1991 to 2 July 1991.

Roberts, C. and Burghes, L. (1995). *Lone parents: scare in the community. Britain in a moral panic*. Community Care. London: Reed Business Publishing

Rowlingson, K. and McKay, S. (1998). *The growth of lone parenthood: diversity and dynamics*. London: Policy Studies Institute

Ruxton, S. (1996). *Children in Europe*. London: NCH Action for Children

Shaw, J. (1997). 'Family Violence and Women's Rights: neutralising violence under the Family Law Reform Act, *Polemic*, Volume 8, Issue 1

Sherman, J. (1998). CSA re-think will scrap complex payment system. *The Times*, 10 February

Shrimsley, R. (1997). 'CSA blunders would take a year to mend.' *Daily Telegraph*, 6 November

Simpson, B., McCarthy, P. and Walker, J. *Being there – fathers after divorce*. Newcastle: Relate Centre for Families Studies

Speed, M. and Kent, N. (1995). *Child Support Agency: national client satisfaction survey 1995*. London: HMSO

Speed, M. and Seddon, J. (1996). *Child Support Agency: national client satisfaction survey 1994*. London: Department of Social Security

Thatcher, M. (1990a). The First National Children's Home George Thomas Society Annual Lecture, January.

Thatcher, M. (1990b). Pankhurst Lecture to the 300 Group, speech to the National Children's Home, July.

United Nations (1997). *UN Demographic Yearbook, 1995*, New York: United Nations

United Nations (1998). *World population monitoring, 1995*, New York: United Nations

Walker, D. (1998). Wanted: a defender for Whitehall's wiley ways. *Independent*, 22 May